Laypeople Into Action

Joseph Cardijn

Laypeople Into Action

Joseph Cardijn

Preface by Edward Mitchinson

Translated by Anne Heggie

Adelaide

This book first appeared under the title *laïcs en premieres lignes, published by editions universitaires 1963*.

© Translation, 1964, first published in that year by geoffrey chapman ltd.

Nihil obstat: joannes m. T. Barton s.T.D., L.S.S., Censor deputatus. Imprimatur: georgius l. Craven, epus, sebastopolis, vig. Gen., Westmonasterii, die 26a feb. 1964.

ISBN:	978-1-925643-24-4	Laypeople into action	soft
	978-1-925643-25-1	Laypeople into action	hard
	978-1-925643-26-8	Laypeople into action	epub
	978-1-925643-27-5	Laypeople into action	pdf

Published by:

An imprint of the ATF Press Publishing
Group owned by ATF (Australia) Ltd.
PO Box 504
Hindmarsh, SA 5007
ABN 90 116 359 963
www.atfpress.com
Making a lasting impact

Acknowledgments

This book was first published under the title *Laics En Premieres Lignes* in 1963, by Editions Universitaires, Paris.

Quotations from Scripture are in the Revised Standard Version.

Contents

Part Four: Laypeople into Action

Preface

Edward Mitchinson

Former National Chaplain of the Young Christian Workers

A significant number of priests, and bishops too, in practically every country, would rate Mgr Joseph Cardijn as the biggest single human influence on their pastoral ideas and attitudes.

Laypeople would go further. Like the multitudes in St John's vision, a number past all counting from every race and tongue would gratefully ascribe their Christian way of life, their very belonging to the Church, their life-long Christian commitment, to Cardijn and the movement he founded. Setting out to found one movement, he has inspired a hundred others in the Church and beyond it. The Young Christian Worker movement was the unswerving object of his zeal; the whole lay apostolate has benefited from his vision. If his approach and method were unique, their very terms have now become the accepted parlance of the modem apostolate. Today the laity are moving into their own in the Church. Cardijn has contributed perhaps more than any other priest to this.

Joseph Cardijn was born into a Flemish working family on 18 November 1882. In 1912, when he was curate in a suburb of Brussels, he formed the first group of young workers in a movement which has since developed world-wide proportions: Cardijn's answer to the problem of dechristianisation is to insert the whole of Christianity into the whole of life. Fifty years of commitment to this end, through a practical program of apostolate, have made Cardijn a precursor of Pope John's *aggiornamento*. It is not difficult to see his influence on all the most profound stirrings in the Church of the last forty years, and in the changes which Vatican II is bringing about.

If I may quote from an article which puts this very neatly:

Mgr Cardijn has never claimed to be a theologian. But it is difficult to exaggerate the extent to which he has stimulated theological reflection . . . Since the war, the treatise on the Church has been enriched with a most important chapter, hitherto unsuspected, on the theology of the laity, and the whole world knows how much this owes to the Young Christian Worker movement . . . Cardijn's repeated insistence on the special and irreplaceable role of the laity, on the need for an organised lay apostolate, may seem trite to many of today's young theologians. We must not forget that it is largely thanks to him that they have become truisms, for they express an intuition which he was one of the first to perceive with intensity . . . Did people, before him, talk of the theology of work? . . . His is the credit for realising, before it was generally accepted, and for repeating endlessly, that man is an incarnate being, that we are not here to save souls, but to lead people to God, body and soul, together with their whole environment . . . It was another of his innovations to dare to think in terms of the mass, without ever forgetting that the mass is made up of persons, who must be treated as free individuals, with respect for their personalities. The present thought and the present life of the Church would not be what they are and would not have the vitality that all agree that they do have, if we had not profited from his perception and prophetic dynamic energy.[1]

A course of Cardijn's dialectic would be the best remedy for the fears and hesitations with which some of the Council's changes have been received. The Church is not frozen, fixed and paralytic; she is the living, growing, transforming body of Christ. The good and desirable change is the one that is the fruit of a dialectic between reality and faith, between how things really are and how God wants them to be. The Church's life must be a continued incarnation, a Christian transformation of reality, a Christian revolution of hearts and lives. It is this dialectic method of Cardijn's which Pope John, in *Mater and Magistra*, took up and proposed to all as the best method of socio-religious education and apostolate.

---

1. Roger Aubert, in *Hommage à Cardijn*, Brussels, 1963.

This is, and looks like remaining, the only book Cardijn has written. That he should have written it at ail, and then at the age of eighty-two, is something of a surprise, for his characteristic means of communication has always been the personal interview, a spoken meditation from the altar, round the table at meetings and what he would term his 'fire-works' from the rally platform. A fine selection of his lectures and addresses has been published in English in Challenge to Action; the contents of that book were originally addressed to Young Christian Worker audiences. This present book is addressed to all interested in the lay and social apostolate.

If I may add a personal impression, I see Cardijn as a small, neat, cassocked figure, with a rather puckish face, drawn in alternate lines of thoughtful concentration, which tell of the obsession of his life, and of a smile that accompanies his message of Christ's love for the poorest, the most lowly of the workers. The short crew cut of hair, now white, adds to the dynamic, rather electric quality of his appearance.

At a study week or international conference, when he turns round before Mass and gives a spoken meditation, eyes closed as he slowly suggests thoughts for reflection, you know that he has been up at least an hour before-hand in prayer. He will pour out his heart for an hour at a time with fervent oratory on the human and divine dignity of young workers, and the glory of their mission, but in private life and conversation he will waste no single or idle word. At lunch-time during conferences, while the sweet is being served, he will slip quietly away, and by the time we are getting up from coffee, Cardijn has had his rest and is back at work at his desk. Whatever the occasion, he retires at night as soon as politeness permits, for prayer and rest in preparation for the Lord's work on the morrow. Such personal discipline is part of the secret of his unflagging zeal and generous readiness to undertake and carry through one vast missionary journey after another.

When this journeying is at an end, those who cannot hear him will be grateful for this book, through which 'his sound will go forth into all the earth and his words unto the ends of the whole world'.

Edward Mitchinson
24 March 1964.

Foreword

At the End of the Road

I have devoted the whole of my priestly life to the lay apostolate, but I have had to wait until today—the eve of my eightieth birthday—for the opportunity of publishing something about it.

For many years I have wanted to make a searching study of the necessity of this apostolate and the way it could best be realised in practical life. The problem that this sets the young workers has attracted me since my adolescence, but I have always seen it as part of a whole vision of the laity and its needs and resources. This has always been an obsession with me. Ever since my first ventures I have become more passionately involved in it. And after so many missionary journeys in so many continents, the problem of the laity and of the formation and organisation that are absolutely necessary for the future of the Church and of the world seems to me increasingly to be a universal and fundamental one. For the older I get, the more I am convinced that the importance of the lay apostolate is a decisive factor in the future of the world and the salvation of humanity. This is why I came to collect together the many notes I have written about this subject during more than fifty years of activity as a priest. They are reflections arising from everyday apostolic life which develop the theme I have never tired of repeating to the young people of the YCW: 'Each young worker, each working girl has a divine destiny and a divine mission, beginning not after death, but from today, in the conditions of their everyday life, where they are the first and immediate apostles of God in their environment and among their comrades.' This affirmation, which inspired the birth and the belief of the YCW, does not belong to it alone. It is part of the very essence of Christianity and applies to the whole conception of the Christian laity.

I have often repeated that this is the whole dialectic of Christianity, which is in reality the reply to the Marxist dialectic. The thesis of this dialectic is that every person born into the world has a divine destiny and mission; all people are God's apostles among other people. This fundamental truth has inspired thousands of laypeople to apostolic action; it has charged their lives with truly religious meaning and sent them out to the ends of the earth. It has given birth to a whole spiritual conception of life, inspired by faith in God as creator and redeemer, which draws all people to participate in the one and only apostolate—that of Christ.

The thesis is inseparable from its historical antithesis, which is the human persons' act of refusal to God's plan of love. This refusal is made up of ignorance, indifference and an accumulation of opposition, struggles, difficulties and obstacles which stand in the way of the realisation of the divine plan and play an important part in the history of humanity.

This is why God's plan of love can only be fulfilled if the Christian dialectic develops towards its end in a continually new synthesis, always better adapted to its purpose, always spreading and expanding, until at last it is universal: the movement of the lay apostolate, willed by God, lived by the example of Christ, guided and animated by the Church, and spread among all people to the ends of the earth and the consummation of the world.

These notes are the outcome of a long spiritual journey: an idea which has been put into practice and lived.

The movement did not forge straight ahead towards its goal without wavering, nor were there clearly defined stages in the formulation of an idea developing resolutely towards its conclusion. On the contrary. The movement has often gone backwards and forwards; there have been many regressions and a thousand fresh starts and lengthy processes of trial and error—both in expression and in practical application—but it never ceases to reach out towards its great goal which is both far off and yet daily very close. The challenge is this:

> How can people, all people, be made aware that they have
> a mission on earth that God himself has entrusted to them
> from the very moment of the creation and the redemption,
> a mission the Church proclaims to them and helps them to
> realise? What can be done to make each person live with

this unshakable conviction: 'God needs me! I am God's missionary'?

This mission given by God to all of humanity finds its fullest expression in the lay apostolate. It consists in building a world according to God's will, 'a fraternal humanity where the humble are loved and helped by their brothers',[2] witness to the presence and the life of God, for the establishment of this kingdom of peace and glory. The following pages, then, are not an argument or a methodical account of the whole problem; nor, by any means, do I claim to lay down a finished doctrine, a hard and fast method, and a perfect apostolic style. I am not a teacher, a theologian, a canon lawyer or a writer, but a man of action, always on the move, always searching and enquiring *'Quaerite et invenietis . . . Quaerite primum regnum Dei*—Seek and ye shall find . . . Seek ye first the Kingdom of God . . .' (Luke 12:22).

After fifty years, 'Seek . . .' is still my motto.

In the exercise of my ministry as a priest, I have been what people call a great traveler. And the more I have travelled through towns and countries, the more clearly have I seen that the lay apostolate is the vital factor in the permanent confrontation of the Church with the needs of the present world. It is through laypeople that the Church is in the world, and the more technical and unified our universe becomes, the more pressing will be the need for real lay apostles. If the world's most urgent problems are not studied and resolved in the light of the Christian dialectic I outlined earlier, we are moving towards a catastrophe for humanity and for the Church.

I have always been struck by the contacts I have had with non-Catholics, non-Christians, and people who are either a-religious or anti-religious. Each time they have brought home to me more forcefully the fact that Christian laypeople, if they exercise a true, deep and vital apostolate, can and must bring a positive solution to the problems of the modern world.

I am also convinced that the lay apostolate—whether it is active in a specifically religious or specifically secular field—will never attain the development and efficiency that are absolutely necessary for the world that is coming into being if the clergy and those who educate the laity do not see, on the one hand, what is man's original, essential

---

2. Speech of Pius XII at the *World Conference of the YCW*, in Rome, 25 August 1957.

mission on earth and, on the other, what laypeople in the Church must do to help all of humanity discover and fulfil this mission.

The basic formation which each Christian and each individual needs will depend on the clarity of this vision. The action which must be carried out will be closely linked to this formation, and for this formation and action there must be organisation and suitable institutions, both in the Church and in the secular world. Formation, action, organisation, united and inseparable, producing a ferment, a leaven, in and for the mass of humanity which must be transformed, influenced and trained.

I have always felt that everything possible should be done in the Church to achieve unanimity in the conception of the mission of each man and each Christian, with all its consequences: unity and organisation which call for the union of action and formation. Thus, all of humanity and all Christians will finally become conscious of, convinced of and united for the realisation of this mission.

The Second Vatican Council will discuss the place and the mission of laypeople in the Church, and will seek means of promoting their indispensable apostolate, as much in the purely religious field as in the secular. Will the study of these questions be limited to the layperson's task only insofar as it touches the Church, with its apostolic and educative consequences? Or will the problem be taken up in all its hum an and earthly dimensions? This second line of discussion would be bound to be immensely valuable, and should answer in particular many of the questions that non-Catholics and non-Christians are asking today. It should even interest the great international institutions, and could be a most valuable guide to the nations who are trying to find their way through the labyrinth of philosophies and ideologies. It should bring about a theology of the Catholic laity, and at the same time provide a very timely opening for all people of goodwill, who could thus discover in the lay apostolate a call to universal co-operation and solidarity.

It is in this context that this book should be read. My aim is not simply to look back on the past, but to stimulate fresh thought and study. From day to day I have experienced the marvellous work of cooperation that the lay apostolate demands, with a very great number of priests and laypeople; and these pages are the outcome of all their combined efforts, on the basis of the experience of the YCW all future study too, should be carried out in common.

The lay apostolate has not yet reached maturity: far from it! Undoubtedly it has never been absent from the life of the Church, and even during the most critical periods it has achieved marvels. But the ultimate stage —that in which priests, religious, and laypeople will all be convinced that religious life and apostolic life are one and the same thing—whether it is a matter of personal sanctification, or action on and with others—that stage is still far off! When its hour strikes, it will mark a glorious date in the history of the Church. And not only in the Church, but in the history of the world. '*Ut unum sint*—That they may be one', said Christ in his prayer at the Last Supper. If these words apply to the unity of all Christian confessions and even of all religions and ideologies, surely they apply also to unity between all people and to the very conception of human life itself: that all should be one in the conception of man's life, in the apostolic mission entrusted to him, and in the cooperation he should bring through his life to the work of the creation and the redemption?

For the lay apostolate can and must realise this unity, with respect to all consciences, races and cultures; in the brotherhood of mutual aid between all peoples, classes and individuals; in the union of all efforts for the promotion of the humblest and poorest and the comfort and consolation of all people.

In bringing about unity, the lay apostolate will contribute to peace on earth between all people, and to the even more radiant manifestation of the glory of God.

Justice, peace, brotherhood and the glory of God: on earth as it is in heaven'.

Part One
Looking Back

1
The Journey Begins

I have spoken and written a great deal about the lay apostolate. Even before the First World War, when I first began parish work as a curate, I was concerned with study-groups for young working girls and women, factory workers and teachers; with the trade union organisations and co-operative groups; and, above all, with the need to infuse new life, through retreats and days of recollection, into all the parochial movements for apostolic formation.

During the long months I spent in prison in the 1914–18 war I had plenty of time for thought and I was able to jot down a number of notes.

By that time I already had behind me a whole series of incidents, influences, discoveries and studies, which had all impelled me to make daily headway along this path.

My mother played a very large part in my religious formation. Before we went to school, she had taught us all the prayers of the Church, and not only its prayers, but what the Church's life was. She was wonderfully gifted in talking to us in the evening before she put us to bed. It was through her that I learnt Bible history and a great part of the history of the Church, and with her, at home in the family and in the life of our parish, that I gradually began to live the liturgy. From our earliest youth she had taught us to love the poor. No one who came begging was ever ignored.

I was nine years old when *Rerum Novarum* appeared I would need a whole book to tell about how I discovered the problem of the working world and especially of the young workers, who were still children like me. For I was able to go to the seminary to become a priest, instead of going to the factory like my little schoolmates but obviously I could not put them out of my mind.

During my seminary holidays we used to talk about them at home every day, and I used to see groups of them going past morning and evening, on their way to work. Then, to discover for myself how forsaken, neglected and demoralised they were, I travelled around the industrial regions of the country.

When my father died in 1903, I vowed at his death-bed to consecrate myself to the salvation of working youth and the working class. This vow became the guiding motive of my life. I was ordained in 1906, and was able to follow a course of sociology and political science at the University of Louvain. This helped me to rough out a provisional synthesis of facts which I had been aware of since my childhood. Then, during trips to Germany, Holland, England and France, I met the people who were having such a great influence at that time on the future of the working-class world: the pioneers of the Christian Workers' Movement of München-Gladbach; Baden Powell, the founder of the Scout movement; Leon Harmel, the organisers of *Semaines Sociales de France*, and the leaders of the *Sillon*; and the leaders of English trade unionism. To these journeys and contacts I should add the researches which I carried out in different parts of French-speaking Belgium during my five years teaching at the junior seminary of Basse-Wavre.

In 1912, Providence, speaking through religious authority, took me to the parish of Laeken, where my ministry brought me into direct contact with laypeople and made it possible for me to contribute to their apostolic formation. The first groups of the girls' YCW, then of the boys' YCW itself, began in this way, and then developed and multiplied through the ups and downs common to all new ventures; trial and error, opposition, wavering, and fresh starts.

Cardinal Mercier, without interfering, watched and hesitated. For thirteen whole years, right up until 1925, this venture was striving to adjust itself, both as to its inner orientation and as to how it could best be introduced into the heart of the parochial community and the lay organisations of that time.

Even before the 1914–18 war, when Catholic Action first began to be organised, people wanted to separate it from the other lay apostolate activities (social and political action, youth work, Marian Sodalities, third orders, etc). So it was that I began to define, and then to make known, my own idea of Catholic Action, which, to my mind, has two inherent requirements:

a. Catholic Action is simply a preparation, a school of training, a service and a representative action; it is mandated by the hierarchy to raise up and form laypeople for the apostolate, and to co-ordinate the different forms it takes.

b. Laypeople train and form each other; they realise their own apostolate in their everyday lives and habitual environments, accepting their human condition as it presents itself from day to day; by trying to discover, evaluate and resolve their own problems and those of others; and by achieving, at the very heart of their secular life, the apostolic mission entrusted to them by Christ and the Church.

I have been following this line of thought ever since confirming, developing and narrowing it down to its essentials throughout my experience as a priest. But before I begin to tackle a more thorough and searching analysis of my subject, I want quickly to stress here its two essential aspects.

As early as 1920–22, I saw Catholic Action very differently from the way it was organised in those days. People wanted Catholic Action to be one single, general, uniform movement, the same everywhere and for everyone, but I wanted it to be a unifying (and not uniform) co-ordination in the heart of the parochial, diocesan and ecclesiastical community, with a view to the mutual support that lay apostles need. I saw in it certain common aims, of a spiritual and above all temporal order: the participation of everyone in the liturgy and worship, respect for and defence of public morality, the press and the radio, presence in national structures, social action, etc. I saw Catholic Action as essentially specialised and complementary—basically complementary to the priestly apostolate, because it is the work of laypeople in the sense that it prepares them for the real apostolate in everyday life, and specialised in its organisations, which must answer different needs and adapt to different environments.

Essentially specialised, it is also essentially co-ordinated. There are not two kinds of Catholic Action, there are only different fields of application. And because of this, its methods must be *essentially specialised* and conditioned by the age, sex and environment of laypeople, by the problems and conditions of their lives and their specific aims. But Catholic Action should also be essentially unifying, through co-operation and a conception of life which embrace the whole of the Church's mission.

I conceived the organisation and the methods of Catholic Action differently from what actually existed because I considered that *its aim was to christianise the whole of secular life*, both individual and social: this was, to my mind, its starting point and its final end.

In other words, I wanted it to be *totally incarnate*.

This is how I came to be concerned, in the development of my thought in my priestly life, with what I should like to call 'the lay apostolate of laypeople':

> an apostolate peculiar to them, because of their lay state, their lay life, their lay environment, because of the problems arising from their lay vocation and mission.[3]

At the same time, I have always stressed that the lay apostolate and lay organisations are a vital, integral part of the direct mission of the hierarchy and clergy in the work of sanctification and preaching of the gospel, through an active participation in parish life (participation in worship and the sacraments, catechetic activities, etc), and also through their sustained efforts to arrive at a deeper and fuller spiritual and doctrinal understanding by means of retreats, days of recollection and other means of renewing the spiritual life.

The most enthusiastic pages in the history of the YCW, for instance, have been those of the Easter campaigns that were carried out in factories, stations and public transport, in working-class suburbs and homes; the liturgical campaigns for a more active participation in the mass through the use of the missal and the practice of dialogue mass; the sacramental campaigns which aimed at a greater understanding of the meaning and importance of baptism, confirmation and marriage. And all this was done not theoretically, not by talk which left the young workers passive, but through actions and activities for which they were themselves responsible and in which they really had to live their convictions in order to transmit them to their comrades.

My basic concern has always been to bring religion back to the surroundings of real life and the problems these raise. This is where laypeople must be what Pius XI calls 'the first and immediate apostles'. This is where they have their own irreplaceable apostolate. Their

---

3. It is this aspect of the lay apostolate that I am dealing with in this book, without forgetting the other aspects. The whole of Part III deals extensively with the formation necessary for the entire lay apostolate.

whole lay life should become an apostolate, and for this they must be united with Christ and the Church. It is the whole Church in a state of mission.

It is not a matter of humanising environments before christianising them, nor of first changing structures. We are concerned with the christianising of individual people. The lay apostolate is not primarily a temporal action; it is essentially an evangelising action working through the environments and problems of life. This evangelising action must be united with the hierarchy and the priesthood, whose own form of apostolate it prepares and continues. Involvement with this movement in secular life certainly doesn't exclude any other preoccupation: the number of religious, priestly, contemplative and missionary vocations that have been inspired by the YCW is the most eloquent witness of this.

It was through discovering and studying the life of the young workers that I came to concern myself with the specific apostolate of laypeople, and began to think about the problems relating to work, working-class institutions and the whole of working-class life, and from there I came to consider all secular institutions.[4]

The YCW, as I have said before, has always pro- claimed from the very beginning that *each young worker has a divine vocation and mission specific to himself, in his life and his working environment.* This divine mission is essential and irreplaceable. It is the very basis of his rights and duties, as well as being the means of raising the whole working-class world. The realisation of this mission is absolutely essential to the very life of the Church.[5]

From this personal mission, made incarnate in the life of all young workers, stems the mission of the apostolic movement which must unite them, help them, form them and speak in their name, with a view to this very mission itself.

It was through analysing and experimenting with the young workers' apostolate, which was backed and inspired by the YCW, that I began to advocate the advancement of all laypeople and lay apostolate movements in the Church and in the world.

---

4. Bear in mind that 'lay' and 'secular' are both words whose ambiguity does not facilitate a clear understanding of ideas. I shall come back to this later.
5. Pope Pius XII emphasises this several times in his address to the YCW, in 1957, which I have already quoted.

This means that I believe in the necessity of evaluating the apostolic mission of all the laypeople in the Church of stressing the importance of each individual human destiny and the value of each man's life on earth—if we are to solve the problems set by creation and the redemption.

The field of the Church, then, must be enlarged to reach the whole of humanity, while all people are being made aware of the grandeur of their human mission, with the responsibility and the educative demands that this implies.

This is why, in my continual effort to explain their mission to laypeople, I have never started with the Church and her mission, in which the layperson's mission must be included. I have always started with lay life and problems, with the mission of each man on earth and the apostolic significance of his life. Whenever I approached the workers, young people or adults, in my parish ministry, my first questions were always: 'Where do you live? Where do you work? How much do you earn? Have you got enough time to see your children and to educate them?' and not, as some of them pointed out to me: 'Do you go to mass? What Catholic organisation do you belong to?' What is more, starting with the vital questions that make up the stuff of human life has enabled me to talk with non-Christians: Buddhists, Hindus, Moslems, agnostics, socialists, communists, etc.

For every human being is called by God, Christ and the Church, because all people, historically, belong to the order of grace and redemption. Many do not listen to or do not hear this call, but nearly all have an intuition, a confused consciousness of it. No one is entirely cut off from it.

It is along these broad lines that thought and experience deepened and developed, meanwhile taking shape in the organic growth of the YCW. This movement, which had already become a reality, was due to be presented to the highest authority of the Church.

I was able to be in Rome at the beginning of 1925 and I had the providential grace to be received in private audience by Pope Pius XI, who gave his approval to the aim, method and organisation of the YCW[6] This first meeting with the Holy Father was the beginning

---

6. During my months in prison in the 1914–18 war, I drafted the main outlines of what appeared in 1925 under the title 'Manuel de la JOC'.

of the long dialogue in which Pius XI and his successors assured the growth and the future of the YCW in the world.

The pontificate of Pius XI was dominated by a very great thought: the Church must be rooted in the realities of life. Everyone is aware of the far-reaching developments he instigated during that time concerning the clergy, the native episcopate, missionary action, the social question, the laity and Catholic Action. This line of thought was sustained and spread by the great encyclicals.

These were also the days in which Fascism held the whole of Italian life, and the youth in particular, in its grip. Nazism was rising like a flood-tide. It was then that Pius XI said: 'Whoever touches Catholic Action attacks the most vital organism of the church.' In 1929 and 1931 he officially received 1,500 young workers and as many young working girls delegated by the YCW of Belgium, and explained their mission to them: 'You are the missionaries of the Church in the world of work.'

In 1935 the YCW, which had officially been in existence for ten years, saw its first appearance on the international scale. By this time the principles and methods on which the movement was based had been perfected in essentials, and Pius XI solemnly gave it official sanction, declaring it to be 'an authentic form of Catholic Action, perfectly adapted to the present time.'[7] Thus the first step was made : the combination of all these events resulted in an initial synthesis which, although far from complete, contained the germ of all subsequent developments.

---

7.   Signed letter of Pius XI to Cardinal Van Roey, 19 August 1935.

2

The Lay Apostolate: A Vital Necessity in the Church[8]

The further we penetrate the living reality of Catholic Action, the more aware we become of the marvelous resources the lay apostolate brings to the Church, and the better we can understand the moving insistence of the Holy Father who wants Catholic Action to become the participation of laypeople in the hierarchical apostolate everywhere in the Church.

If we simply stop short at the juridical constitution of Catholic Action, or are content with an external or superficial analysis of its theoretical concept, we can have no idea of the extraordinary renewal stirring and kindling within it nor of the transformation it is working in the lives of the faithful. Nor are we the astonished witnesses of the conquests and victories Catholic Action is bringing about. And we run the risk of remaining outside it of being indifferent, or indeed even skeptical and distrustful, before the spiritual and apostolic rebirth which is being revealed among young people especially

---

8. Chapters II and III of this book appeared in 1935 in two articles in 'Notes de Pastorale Jociste'. The original text has undergone only minor changes; the reader himself can bring them up to date as far as the terminology, practical applications and concrete forms in general are concerned. If I had to write these articles today, I should doubtless use other terms but for me their essential content has not changed. Several elements, which have been verified by experience, are defined more clearly.

I should like to repeat that in insisting on the absolute necessity, for the Church and the world, of this 'formally constituted apostolate of the laity to the laity', which in 1935 was called 'Catholic Action', I do not wish in any way to diminish the importance of the apostolate which the layperson is called to exercise in the Church in preparing, supporting and continuing priestly action. It is obvious that the ideas developed in these two chapters presuppose the unity of the apostolate in the Church; this is made very clear in Chapter VIII.

and which must awaken vast expectation in the heart of every priest and militant Christian.

Have we understood and reflected enough on the place of the lay apostolate in the Church; for there is in the Church an apostolate which truly belongs to the laity, an apostolate which transforms lay life into apostolic life. You have to see it at work in concrete situations and in actual experience to witness with astonishment and delight the actions—nearly always humble, concealed, and often heroic—of young men and girls who are transforming their lives into an apostolate of extraordinary fruitfulness: only then can you understand the great riches that result from this for the Church which, without them, would be unable to achieve anything in this basic sphere of her influence.

Their everyday working life becomes a missionary life; their engagements the magnificent novitiate of a sublime vocation. When we say: 'Without work, there is no host, no wine, no paten, no chalice, no altar, no mass; without work there is no church, and no religion, not only have we stated a material fact, but a great spiritual truth. When we say: 'Without Christian homes there are no priests, no religious, no missionaries, no apostles', not only are we emphasising the apostolic importance of Christian love in marriage, but at the same time revealing to young people who are preparing to marry the apostolic significance of the need for affection and love which is awakening in their hearts.

What practical applications for the education of young people become apparent when lay life is seen to have apostolic meaning. What a thrilling vision of life it creates in them, what a driving force against temptations! And above all what terrific resources and unfailing energy an ordinary lay life, apostolically transformed, offers to the Church!

It is of paramount importance not to forget that lay life, on the level of family, profession, feelings, etc. is and always will be the raw material of Catholic Action, material which first and foremost must be transformed apostolically. The first and immediate apostles of workers will be workers', said the Pope in *Quadragesimo Anno*. The first and immediate apostolate of laypeople to laypeople is the basic material of Catholic Action.

If we forget this truth, we lose sight of the priority of values, we stop short at artificial, arbitrary methods of formation and action which will never come to grips with real, everyday life. The Christian transformation of all the environments of daily life—schools, work, leisure, travelling, family—the conquest of the masses of people leading ordinary lives in this daily environment is the raison d'être of the lay apostolate. This lay apostolate is as different from the priestly apostolate as the lay state and lay life are different from the priestly state and life.

Once again, we must not look at this difference superficially or we will underestimate it and fail to understand all that the lay apostolate brings to the Church because of this difference.

A priest can not take part in the apostolate which really belongs to laypeople because of his priestly state and life. He isn't fitted to it. But it is his task to make sure that laypeople receive the necessary graces to achieve this apostolate. This is what his priestly ministry is. He gives Christ to the layperson; the person of Christ, the grace of Christ, the doctrine of Christ. He helps the layperson to make Christ incarnate in their lay life, so that they become a radiant witness in their whole environment—'*Mihi vivere Christus est*—For me, to live is Christ' (1 Phil 1:21).

Then the mystical Christ becomes a marvelously varied reality. Christ is truly everywhere, at every moment, in all people, all environments and all conditions of life. The Church is truly everywhere when all its members live in this way the life of Christ and his Mystical Body. What a driving force for penetration and transformation!

The lay apostolate, then, is complementary to the priestly apostolate because it is different from it, dependent on it, and auxiliary, in the true sense of the word. It is an indispensable complement to the priestly apostolate, which can only achieve its end fully and completely if laypeople are faithful to their own apostolate. When this happens, the Mass offered by the priest at the altar will become a Mass prolonged on all those altars of secular life: the worktable, the loom, the lathe, the joiner's bench, the typist's desk . . . The *Gloria* and *Sanctus* will rise in praise not only from the Church but from Christian lives which have become a prayer, an atonement, an act of grace. And all the environments of secular life will be transformed into temples where laypeople truly render glory to God.

When we consider the lay apostolate in this light, acting on the raw material which is the layperson's own life, we begin to understand how it must be adapted in order to be really potent and powerful.

Adapted to his or her life, it must take in the circumstances of his or her environment, the profession he or she practices, the role he or she plays, the problems he or she has to resolve, and their sphere of influence. Seen in this way, all the elements of the lay persons' life become truly apostolic. For life is not uniform, any more than society is, but the two cannot be separated. In the same way, the Church and Catholic Action are inseparable, in spite of and perhaps due to the adaptation that is needed in the apostolate. This adaptation will be all the more essential because Catholic Action must act on the raw material of the apostolate, which is life itself. Where more external, more secondary forms of action are concerned, the need for adaptation seems less obvious. But one shouldn't have illusions about these activities; they will never give real, lasting results unless they are grafted on to a vital apostolate which aims at what life really is. How many apostolic ventures in which more external, noisy and spectacular methods are used will seem momentarily to produce astonishing results, and then leave nothing behind them but bitter disappointment because they did not take up and transform real lay life.

It is then that we will see that the lay apostolate and Catholic Action are irreplaceable in and for the Church. Woe to him who underestimates them or mocks at them! He understands neither the mystery of the Church nor the mystery of the Redemption. The priest cannot and must not replace laypeople in their apostolic mission; he must teach them about this mission, and assure them of the graces they need.

The layperson is irreplaceable! What a proof of divine love and Christian dignity this is. When the young worker has understood that he has a unique role to fill in the Church, in the apostolate, his difficult and humble state of life becomes dear to him. And then, what a driving force, what holy ambition he is fired with! This is the secret of the YCW This is largely how its mystique was born. And when we succeed in awakening souls to a consciousness of their task, we can expect miracles.

These are the five features of a primary, fundamental Catholic Action: an apostolate peculiar to laypeople—different from the priestly apostolate, but complementary to it—adapted and irreplaceable. If we list these features together we can understand how absolutely essential this apostolate is to the Church:

— it is a necessity which is not based on arbitrary ideas; it is not optional or secondary, but a primary necessity;

— it is a necessity which is due not simply to an insufficient number of priests, but to the very insufficiency of the priestly apostolate, which is not the whole Catholic apostolate;

— it is a necessity which does not result only from the danger of modem secularisation, but is rendered more acute, serious, and urgent by this;

— it is an eternal necessity for the Church, from her beginning to her end, in all countries and all centuries, because of its very constitution and divine mission;

— it is a necessity which does not have an ecclesiastical origin, but which is of the divine order, willed by God himself.

And so we can say that the lay apostolate belongs to the very essence of the Church. Laypeople belong to the Church inasmuch as they participate in her apostolate. The Church too is apostolic in and through her laypeople.

There can be no sheep without a shepherd, no shepherd without sheep. All together, each one in his own place, they take part in Christs apostolate. The head cannot be separated from the members, any more than the members can be separated from the head: the whole of the Mystical Body must be apostolic. Neither clericalism nor laicism but living unity.

The very nature of the Church demands an apostolate of the laity. all the concordats signed under the pontificate of Pius XI refer to the liberty of Catholic Action as an integral part of the liberty of the Church.

It is because the lay apostolate is so important that the efforts to promote it have been so urgent. This is especially so in the modem world, where the Church has to meet and cope with the invasion of secularisation. The Church, too, must explain the nature of Catholic Action and the characteristics belonging to it. One of the movement's features must be a certain formality, since it is an organised lay apostolate. It is organised under the direction of religious authority, which must both be responsible for it and, at the same time, help it to attain its maximum development and to achieve its real aim. A living, disciplined, adapted organisation, under the unifying authority of the hierarchy. Today, when life and living environments are influenced by currents and movements which go beyond the narrow framework of parishes or localities, Catholic Action must increasingly be organised on a national and international scale, so that it can act on public opinion and set in motion methods of action and formation which will inspire confidence and increase its forces. Most important, the doctrine and action of the Church must be brought to bear on all human problems.

The organisation of Catholic Action must be hierarchical. This is valid from two points of view. Looked at from the outside, Catholic Action is completely de pendent on the pontifical and episcopal hierarchy. Seen from within, its very organisation demands a lay hierarchy which will ensure unity between all parties and activities, stir up a glowing, confident, enthusiastic impetus for every campaign and assert the authority of the representatives of Catholic Action, both in government and non-government institutions and in the Church. Thus the collaboration of the laity with the hierarchical apostolate will grow and be strengthened twofold within the Church. There will be a disciplined laity, with its own organisation—'acies ordimta—in battle array'— conscious of its responsibilities; each member freely, proudly and fully subject to the hierarchy, in his rank, in his place, in his environment, joyfully participating in the apostolate which belongs to his Church with all the means and methods at his disposal.

Catholic Action, then, is the lay apostolate mandated by the hierarchy, that is officially commissioned by religious authority. Not that each layperson in Catholic Action has an official mandate; but the organisation bears this mandate, and all its members to some extent participate in it. It is the militants and leaders, however, who take part most effectively in the execution of this mandate and train members to understand the mission with which the Church has entrusted them in their organisation. When a militant has understood this, we obtain unheard-of results. We can demand sanctity, perfection, discernment and competence of laypeople in the world, just as we demand them of religious. Once again, what a powerful impetus this gives them!

Those who win members and spread the organisation,[9]—leaders and militants—are the educators, the heads, the true representatives of Catholic Action in their organisation; it opens a vast field of apostolic action to these laypeople who are genuine missionaries, and

---

9. Pius XI calls them 'the multipliers'.

who without leaving their lay life or escaping from their environment become the true carriers of the Gospel, the authorised representatives of the Church. And the fruitfulness of their apostolate will continue to be a pledge of progress and a consolation to the Holy Father.[10]

These considerations appear particularly appropriate in helping laypeople to understand more fully their indispensable place and magnificent role in the Church. They are truly the 'chosen race', the 'holy nation, the royal priesthood', of which St Peter speaks (1 Peter 2:9). Their role is not a passive one but an active one, in which they must take upon themselves the responsibility belonging to them in the Church and in the world.

---

10. We find this significant passage in *Quadragesimo Anno* (1931): 'We have been overjoyed to see the dense hosts of young Christian workers who have risen to the call of divine grace and cherish the noble ambition of reconquering the souls of their brothers for Christ . . .'

3
The Working Class Apostolate—One Practical Realisation of the Lay Apostolate

The importance of the lay apostolate, both for the Church and for society, can only be fully understood if all its features are related to the working class laity. The Christian solution to the working class question and, to a great extent, the social question, is to be found here.

When we think about the high percentage of workers in the total population, of those hundreds and thousands of wage-earners and working class families, the task facing the workers' apostolate is staggering. *Quadragesimo Anno*, and today, *Mater et Magistra*, cannot be understood unless we realise what the working class laity can do. This is, moreover, the only way of setting the whole problem in the light of Christian truth.

The aim of the workers' apostolate can be put under three headings:

a. the transformation of working life
b. the transformation of the working class environment and the system which creates it
c. the transformation of the mass of the workers. The combination of these three inseparable endeavoursis the Catholic solution to the working class problem.

Transformation of the workers' everyday life

The worker, his family and the whole working class are the indispensable partners of God, Christ and the Church in the work of creation and redemption. Such is the order of Providence. The whole of working class life—everywhere and always—has apostolic significance.

I cannot repeat this often enough: while every day human beings are creating new material goods, their professional life is a prayer, a sacrifice, a prolonged mass; it is a vocation and an apostolate. The worker is a witness, a missionary and a sort of catechist, both in and through their life of work. Work is not a punishment, a curse, or a kind of slavery, it is collaboration with the Creator and Redeemer. At his place, in his work, the worker is the first minister, the immediate and intimate collaborator with God.

What a renewed conception of the life of work! What a transformation and revolution this brings to the lowliest and hardest form of work!

Practical implications, too, can be inferred from this mystical conception of the life of work in the professional, social and economic field regarding the code of work and professional ethics and reorganisation. all the changes that are brought about solely through personal gain, competition, violence, hate or passion, will stand condemned forever. Every atheistic, neutral or materialistic doctrine is opposed to this aspect of Catholic doctrine which, far from copying the Marxist doctrine, is often plagiarised by it on all those points that have drawn the workers to Socialism. Each time that I have expounded these positive aspects of the Church's doctrine to working class audiences who are hostile to the Church and even to religion, there has been a delighted response. The workers are not machines, beasts of burden or slaves—they are the sons, the collaborators the heirs of God! What a glorious revelation this is to the family life of the lowliest workers should be see as an apostolic life. To give the Church and the nation the priests, missionaries and apostles they need, to multiply the number of Gods chosen people, to help the Church to spread: this is the ideal that every working class family must have. It is an ideal that can inspire generosity, devotion, self-sacrifice and self-denial, but it also makes social demands.

Now if from this apostolic conception of the family we can arrive at practical conclusions regarding wages, housing and the work of the married woman, and if we understand how the whole organisation of production should be directed towards the broadening and enriching of family life and the life of *every* working class family, isn't this the only really beneficial stand that we can take against *laissez faire* and individualism on the one hand, and all the forms of state socialism, collectivism, and materialistic nationalism on the other?

But it must also be understood that this ordinary, everyday working life, with all its most secular aspects, cannot be separated from religious life; religion must give people an idea, an understanding of life and ways in which it can be applied, which will involve the whole of working class life. Every religious practice and institution—prayer, the sacraments, mass, communion, the liturgy, religious ceremonies—these are only sources, beginnings, channels of divine life which must transform and sanctify all the aspects and manifestations of working class life and, at the same time, render to God the homage of the whole Church community.

What a transformation of working-class life! Only the workers can carry it out. 'By them, between them, for them.'[11] Others can and must help them. But only they themselves live this life, with its struggles, temptations, difficulties and responsibilities. It is often a real way of the Cross, but it also leads to the resurrection and the ascension. The worker and the working class family who have truly understood this won't want to change their condition; in their working class life they are continuing the mission of Christ the worker. Their lives are essential to the redemption of the world.

A profound transformation of the whole environment

Pius XI lamented in *Quadragesimo Anno* that 'dead matter comes out of the factories made beautiful, while people grow corrupted and degraded there'. And before that, he says: 'I am aghast when I think of the great dangers threatening the morality of the workers, especially the young, and the chastity of women and girls in modem factories; when I think of the obstacles to the solidarity and intimacy of family life that are often imposed by the present system, and above all the deplorable housing conditions'.

The working class environment in its professional, family and social aspects, corrupted by false ideas, loose morals and the present system, has in its turn become a corrupt influence on all those who live and work there. It is useless to try to influence the workers in artificially created environments like schools, clubs and circles; if educative action is limited to these artificial environments, the working world will never be saved. It is only to be saved within its own,

---

11. This phrase has characterised YCW groups from the very beginning.

familiar, everyday environment; workers must be taught and helped to act there they must transform this environment, conquer it, bring it into harmony with the providential plan. Now, this transformation can only be wrought from within by those who, like native missionaries, live and work there. Any form of external action will be useless unless it serves to stimulate and to nourish action from within.

The whole working class environment must take on a new meaning, a new sanctifying, humanising, educative value. The home, the factory, the office, the workshop, the worker s district, the train, the bus—all these must become temples and sanctuaries, schools of holiness and honour and moral grandeur.

The worker's environment is the most exposed, and therefore the most important sector of the battlefront of Catholic Action and the lay apostolate. The struggle there is incessant, worse than a battle in the trenches with bombs and poison gas. The souls of al of humanity are in far greater danger than their bodies. To be on the defensive is not enough, it is absolutely essential to take the offensive. It I not enough to put the crucifix back on the wall, Christ must be present in the morality and way of working, as well as in the whole plan and organisation of the family and work environment.

And above all, this must not be limited in application to purely spiritual matters; the necessity of material, temporal applications has to be faced; and it is in this light that we must consider the problems of housing, hygiene, public safety, education, vocational guidance, the rationalisation of work, trade unions, and many others. It is not the Church's business to propose and impose technical solutions; she must inspire, encourage and guide them so that they become a means to the christianisation of the environment and the spreading of Christian life in and through it. The encyclicals on marriage and education should be re-read in this spirit.

The transformation of the mass of workers

Do we think enough about this mass? Are we haunted and obsessed by the thought of these countless multitudes upon whom Christ had compassion and for whom he died? We can be deceived by full churches, by the sight of crowds of people on important feast days, on pilgrimages and in processions. Certainly the majority of the working mass is baptised, and the Church still presides over funerals. But what about their everyday life? Here there is pervasive ignorance, indifference, and a lack of religious consciousness. Unless we are on our guard, the mass will become a-religious, and this danger can only grow greater as a consequence of purely material technical progress.

Once again, though, it must be stressed that the masses can only be reached effectively through militants who live among them, catechists of the masses who share their life and belong to their environment. The problem of the elite and the masses is that of the leaven and the yeast working in the dough. We need an elite for all environments and all conditions of life, an elite of workers, acting in the mass of workers. When we succeed in awakening this apostolic spirit among the masses we will have instilled the true spirit of Catholicism. The Mystical Body of Christ is there. But we must also have the courage to work out genuine ways of transforming the masses. Theoretical, purely intellectual methods certainly will not work, and on the other hand, we must not be deceived by mass manifestations and stop short at external, superficial forms of action, whether they are carried out by means of the press, radio or cinema or expressed in political or social movements, or in cultural or simply recreational activities. These are often no more than forms of escapism, a kind of opium or a source of delusions. Without disregarding collective means of approach, we must be able to go beyond them through contacts which are more penetrating and personal, contacts which are only possible in humble everyday life, in the familiar working class environment, in the family circle, at work, in all the relationships between the workers. The rest is simply fireworks. A football match can draw a big crowd at certain times and in certain circumstances, but whatever one does, the life of the mass is not there. And yet it is this immense mass which must live a human life and the life of Christ, and collaborate in his redemption. This is how the first and immediate apostolate of working class laypeople presents itself. It will be a lay apostolate organised with a view to this triple transformation, responsible for it and absolutely irreplaceable in it. Thus it will be the indispensable complement of the priestly apostolate.

True Catholic Action in the working class, acting on it and acting from within it, must be understood in this way: this is Catholic Action by the working class organised for this conquest of the masses, that is by the workers apostolate. We can and must help this workers' apostolate from the outside, but we can never take their place there—this would be an artificial substitute. The first and immediate apostles of the workers will be the workers themselves'. No one denies that Catholic Action cannot be just any random organisation, that it must be adapted to its purpose, must be armed against all the difficulties inherent in the conquest. This is certainly a difficult and heroic conquest, but one that can be realised. Not to believe this would be unchristian, and, after the results of the last years, unforgivable. But no one can doubt that more and more inner discipline and more unity is needed here than in any other kind of apostolate.

When will the children of light be as wise as the children of darkness?

This realistic, living conception of the worker's apostolate is the only answer to all the fears of division and separation in Catholic Action. The unity of the Mystical Body of Christ, far from being shaken by such an apostolate, can only become more alive and fruitful as a result. Any other unity, based on uniformity, whether of direction or formation, is deceptive, and not infrequently carries within it the seeds of death, or even death itself.

In order to spread to the maximum her apostolic power, the Church, the Bride of Christ, must possess ways and means of forming and helping all her children to transform all the conditions and environments of life. In the organisation of these methods it is useless to try to follow an artificial and preconceived plan, with a superficial appearance of simplicity. We must have the courage to centre these methods on the very plan of Providence and start from real life, which is so rich and indestructible. Christ must be everywhere through and in his members who must live his life, radiating it in their own lives and environments, and in the masses of people around them. And for this the members of Christ must be recruited, trained and supported for this life, this environment and this mass of people.

Thus, Catholic Action is an educative as well as transforming force. To teach all people to see Christ everywhere, to serve him everywhere, to extend his reign- what a prospect this is for education!

'When you did it to one of the least of these my brethren, you did it to me . . . I was hungry . . . I was thirsty . . .' (Matt 25:31–40) . . . I was unemployed, I lived in a slum, I worked at the bottom of a mine: this is the vision of the Mystical Christ. Every social, political and economic problem takes on religious, apostolic meaning when it is seen in this light. It is useless to adopt the politics of the ostrich and refuse to see critical problems on the pretext of Catholic unity. This would be a fictitious unity. Only true unity can be a dynamic, transforming power, can generate that constructive charity which is the soul and the life of the Mystical Body.

The YCW should be set in precisely this perspective. This is the way in which the movement is striving to prepare the workers' apostolate, which, tomorrow, will enable the Church to christianise the entire working class.

But it is not the destiny of the workers' environment alone which is at stake, it is the destiny of the whole of human society. Internecine struggles must be replaced by co-operation between classes and nations. The great family of humanity must be brought under the leadership of its sole Saviour, Jesus Christ. Over and above material and temporal interests, the rising generation must be guided by spiritual and eternal values. In the Catholic lay apostolate, which must embrace all the classes and nations of the world, the workers' apostolate has its own providential mission.

Between totalitarian atheism, which is the extremist expression of modem secularisation, and the Christian lay apostolate, which must spread the vital, living forces of the militant Church, a gigantic duel is being prepared. The YCW, marching forward with the powerful advance of this lay apostolate, must bring to the Church the most dedicated militants, faithful front line of a new workers' apostolate.

Part Two
Towards a Synthesis of
Facts, Doctrine and Apostolic
Experience

4
Distinctions and Confusions

During the last years people have spoken and written a great deal about the lay apostolate. Perhaps this proves that we have still a long way to go and that many things remain to be defined, made more concrete and, above all, clarified, as much in our doctrinal concepts as in what concerns the problem, the methods and all the practical aspects of the question.

When we begin to think about it, one of the most striking things is the confusion that still reigns about the conception involved, and even about terminology: sometimes we feel as if we are venturing on to quicksand, or groping through some labyrinth where we are in danger of quibbling and over-refinement or of losing our way in a maze of different intellectual viewpoints.

Everyone who is sincerely involved in the study of this question should keep striving with even more determination to eliminate all ambiguities, by dint of patience and an unwavering fidelity to the facts of the situation. What is the actual meaning of the terminology we use? We must be clear about this from the beginning.

In everyday speech the word lay is hardly used, unless by people like theorists, leaders of political parties, and civic authorities, who give it a distinctive meaning that is often coloured by their own particular point of view. For instance, we talk about lay schools, lay institutions (orphanages, groups, etc) lay morality, or a lay conception of science. So the term is ambiguous. Laypeople, non-religious, and is used of civil authority or a non-cleric in public or private life. Sometimes it implies 'war with' religion, the Church, and ecclesiastical authorities.

The word 'apostolate' is also applied by certain people to activities that have no religious content. They will speak of the apostolate of science, or art, or song; they will use it to describe the temperament, the activity and the zeal of a militant championing some movement, or a philanthropist who is patronising some cause (democracy, peace, feminism, the masses, the care of old people or the sick), and, admiring his dedication, they will say: 'So and so is an apostle of such and such a group'. The Church, however, gives a completely different meaning to these two words.

To theologians and canon lawyers, the word lay comes from *laos*, the people, which is used in scripture to designate the People of God. 'Layperson', then, means people who belong to the People of God, people who is member. In recent years especially, theologians have thrown light on this etymology and have deepened its positive significance by explaining what belonging to the People of God really involves—participation in its priesthood and its apostolic mission.

In short, in current theological or ecclesiastical terminology, layperson generally signifies someone who is not a monk or a priest; and where the acts and institutions of the Church are concerned, 'laypeople' means the faithful. How greatly this enriches and renews the conception of the Church and the faithful!

The word 'apostolate' is always taken by the Church in its religious sense; it is an institution, an action, a way of life which is both dependent on God's grace, his call and his consecration, and dependent on the Church, and destined to communicate these things to others. Christ is the unique Apostle; the Pope and the bishops are consecrated and ordained apostles; and laypeople are called by Christ and the bishop, in faith and in charity, through the sacraments. And the apostolate is not only dependent on God—it is the way to God and his kingdom. It is dependent on the Church and the hierarchy and it leads towards them. If I myself use the term laypeople, it is principally because I am dealing with questions about the Church in this book, and I have to make a distinction between priests and religious on the one hand, and laypeople on the other. Otherwise I would talk about 'people/person', or 'the human person', and the 'human apostolate', inasmuch as every man and even everything secular in his life is the work of God and has a part in the divine mission, because it has been given a new value by Christ, God-made-man, and by the Church, his Mystical Body.

Finally, if I talk more about a 'lay apostolate' in the secular, temporal field, in life and in the world, it is because this aspect is most often challenged and confused with social action. This doesn't mean that I have attached or do attach less importance to the purely religious lay apostolate, whether it is active in family life, worship, catechising, and so on.

The apostolate of laypeople—that is, the faithful who have been baptised and confirmed—has always existed in the Church, but from the beginning of this century it has taken on fresh vigour. The various phenomena of the secularisation of society have made this imperative. Since we began experimenting with new methods of action, spreading them, and seeing the ensuing results and disappointments, we have begun to ask questions about the duty of the lay apostolate, its nature, its purpose and the conditions of its growth and expansion While the understanding of the whole conception of the Church is deepening, the fact that all the baptised are called to the apostolate is being proclaimed.

There is still a lack of clear understanding of *the scape and the value of the apostolate*: the whole of secular, temporal life must be an apostolate, and this applies to all people, even non-Christians, because they are called by Christ and the Church. Many people will still not admit this, or will fail to see its importance.

Personally—and I have never ceased repeating this all through my priestly life—my own belief is that the layperson must be an apostle first of all in his own life, that is in the temporal, secular sphere. This is the condition of the authenticity of his witness in other fields: worship, doctrine, the sacraments, etc.

Formation for this apostolate in the temporal field—like the whole of Christian formation—depends on religious authority and is ensured by the educative function of the priesthood and those who co-operate with it. Laypeople are only apostles in the measure in which they are formed, and clericalism doesn't enter into this more than into any other spiritual formation. As for the external activity and the organisation of this apostolate—they do not compromise religious authority, nor can they be accused of clericalism. Insofar as he is a human being- he or she is a scholar, citisen or professional person—the apostle has the same rights and duties as everyone else; but for these people these rights and duties are imbued with apostolic meaning, they are given to the person by God for the spreading of God's kingdom and seen in this light, they are dependent on the Church. But when it comes down to different practical situations and attitudes, how difficult to make distinctions and at the same time strive for unity

However, while stressing the urgent necessity of working towards a clearer understanding of these questions, I only mention them in passing. I have always believed that my own task was a dynamic, pastoral one, and this book is written from that point of view. The doctrinal or juridical aspects are only mentioned to remind us of an essential truth.

My purpose is not to define or to analyse.

Nor do I want to dwell on the difference between the religious and the secular, or to show how the latter is completely autonomous in its order, which implies respect for the human and the divine as much in the temporal as in the eternal order. My purpose is not to explain how and why these two orders are different, not only in the way they are expressed—be it individual or institutional—but in their very essence, the first relating to the natural forces of creation, and the second relating to grace and assumed by the redemption. The natural laws governing all the manifestations of the universe and the life and society of mankind must be studied in themselves: this is the field of physics, chemistry, biology, and other sciences. But the use of all created forces, as well as their discovery and study, is at the service of man, tile whole of mankind and its total destiny. And however material this human bond is, it cannot ignore humanity's supernatural destiny, which begins to be realised in his earthly life even before it reaches completion after death. The natural and the supernatural come from the same God and affect the same man.

Finally, I have not tried to explain the basis of the essential bond linking the apostolate and the hierarchy, the priesthood and the laity. But I shall refer to it as the true mainspring of apostolic grace and its transmission to the entire Christian community and to every man on earth; I will stress how united and inseparable they are in their aim and final end. Defining and analysing falls within the scope of the theologian, but there must be those who are rather like 'the voice crying in the wilderness', whose principal task is to give impetus to the baptised who have been called by the Holy Spirit to the sublime mission of spreading the Kingdom of God on earth, in the humblest, most total obedience to the authority of the Church. Apostolic action, in the light of the Church's doctrine, must be increasingly imbued with the burning inspiration that moved Christ when he contemplated the crowds and had compassion for them . . . because they were harassed and helpless, like sheep without a shepherd' (Matt 9:36).

And so my true, my only goal, will be attained when people are convinced of the immense responsibility awaiting laypeople in the apostolic field, and of the effort which must be made, without waiting a single day more, to give them the opportunity to assume this responsibility completely. There is no lack of labour. The harvest is becoming more and more plentiful. We must march forward with our eyes fixed steadfastly on the goal.

5

The Earthly Mission of Humanity[12]

From the beginning of the account of the creation, the earthly mission of man, and, in him, the mission of all humanity, is expressed by God himself:

> God said: 'Let us make man in our image, after our likeness; and let them have dominion over the fish of the sea, and over the birds of the air, and over the cattle, and over all the earth, and over every creeping thing that creeps upon the earth.' So God created man in his own image, in the image of God he created him, male and female he created them. And God blessed them, and God said to them: 'Be fruitful and multiply, and fill the earth and subdue it, and have dominion over the fish of the sea, and over the birds of the air, and over every living thing that moves upon the earth.' God said: 'Behold, I have given you every plant yielding seed which is upon the face of all the earth, and every tree with seed in its fruit; you shall have diem for food . . .' (Gen 1:26–29).

So the nature of this mission emerges clearly and is defined in practical terms:

In its original form, this chapter appeared in November 1957 in a duplicated article entitled 'The earthly mission of man and humanity and the Lay Apostolate'.

---

12. . In its original form, this chapter appeared in November 1957 in a duplicated article entitled 'The Earthly Mission of Man and Humanity and the Lay Apostolate'.

— man is called to be fruitful and multiply;
— to occupy the whole earth;
— to discover and use all the animal, vegetable mineral riches of the earth;
— to establish his mastery over all created forces;
— to manage all the goods of the earth;
— to discover the Creator through the Creators works and to render homage to the Creator.

From this moment, God addresses humanity as a person created in God's own image and likeness, entrusted by God with the execution of the creative plan, of which God is the principle and the end. In the perspective of the Old Testament, 'the works of creation are the normal environment through which human comprehension recognises its Creator'. How very many times in the Old Testament God comes back to this mission, glorifying it and showering it with his blessings, whether it is a matter of individual people or of his whole people. And how often the patriarchs, prophets and psalmists celebrate its grandeur, beauty and holiness. This divine mandate, freely confided to man and inspired by the Fathers goodness, gives a sacred, religious, apostolic character to the whole of man's earthly existence.

— This mission belongs exclusively to man because he is a human being engaged in secular, temporal activities which, at the same time, make up a divine, spiritual, eternal vocation.
— This mission is absolutely necessary in the execution of God's loving design. In order to manifest himself and make himself known, God freely willed to depend on man's faithfulness and to have confidence in his free response.

In this sense, we can say that humanity cannot be replaced in this mission, because God has willed to use humanity: God needs the collaboration of humanity: work, genius, Social, economic and political activities, activity in science and technology, the use of intelligence and culture.

— It must be realised as well that this mission is fundamental, of prime importance, the essential basis of every mission to come.

And so the mission entrusted by God to humanity at the very moment of the creation constitutes the essential dignity of human nature, of which the Church reminds us every day in the Offertory of the Mass: 'O God, who in a wonderful manner created and ennobled human nature . . ' This nobility, this dignity, begin on earth and in time, to be carried through into heaven and perfected in eternity, face to face with God.

Sinful humanity refused and still goes on refusing the divine mission. Corrupting nature in this way, humanity disturbs the temporal and eternal order of God's loving plan, and in answering the divine confidence with pride and egotism, humanity offends God and introduces sin into the soul—original sin, actual sin, personal and social sin— with all their disastrous consequences, both temporal and eternal.

However, sin has not abolished the fundamental mission; God's loving plan has not changed; it is still the basis of human life and dignity. What is more, sin was the *felix culpa* and *necessarium peccatum*—happy fault and necessary sin'—says the liturgy; it gave God the opportunity of revealing still more deeply the mystery of God's love, by placing the redemption at the heart of creation: 'O God, who in a wonderful manner created and ennobled human nature, and still more wonderfully renewed it . . .' The Word of God, in being made flesh in the womb of the Virgin Mary, and in becoming the Man-God, has merited through his life, death, resurrection and ascension, the expiation and the forgiveness of sins. And more than that, the divinisation of human nature has been made possible through participation in Christ's personal life, his doctrine, his grace and his works. God has willed this new plan of love for the whole of mankind in every age and in every continent. 'A light for revelation to the Gentiles, and for glory to thy people Israel' (Luke 2:32).

This is not a mystery which reaches the human person from afar off, in an abstract way; it is revealed through the most intimate and personal presence of God, for it is Christ's desire truly to live and work in each person—'It is no longer I who live, but Christ who lives in me', says St Paul (Gal 2:20)—he desires all of humanity to be united to him and to form with him his Mystical Body.

This is how the logic of the divine plan works. The Church is born of the redemption and commissioned to bring the person and the life of Christ to all people, united in a Christian, apostolic and missionary community. And in this Church, the hierarchy is named and consecrated by Christ himself. From the Church too, guided and animated by the hierarchy, all Christians derive their apostolic role: they are called to collaborate in the spreading of Christ's reign, and for this they must be radiant witnesses to Christ in their own lives and amongst all their brothers and sisters whom they meet in the course of their life even to the ends of the earth.

The whole of redemptive action, however, does not replace or put an end to the primary human mission given to humanity by God. Christ could stay nailed to the Cross till the end of time, all people could be baptised, could pray and communicate—but this alone does not realise God's loving design in creation.

It is certain that without the redemption continued and perfected in the Mystical Body, all the endeavours of the human race would be disrupted, threatened, doomed to failure, because they are tainted with error and sin. Christ and the Church would undoubtedly help individual Christians, and through them all people, to live by his grace and his doctrine in order to ensure their salvation; without doubt, through this very presence and influence they would enable all human institutions to extend God's kingdom and spread his justice and charity on earth as it is in heaven. But this Christian impetus is not enough in itself, it must be made incarnate in the whole of human life, personal and collective.

In order that life may spread on earth according to God's will and the fundamental plan of his creation, the human person must procreate, and must work: science, technology, economy, education and politics, all are needed. And in order that this human, temporal life may lead to the total happiness of the human race, we need the message and the life of Christ, his love, his conception of life, and the morality and civilisation that they have inspired.

Without separating them, we can therefore make a distinction between man's two vocations: one human and the other divine.

Humanity has a vocation, a human mission, which corresponds directly to God's plan in the creation, but is aided, enlightened and guided by the grace and presence of Christ and sustained by its union with the whole of the Church. This mission, common to all humanity and carried out in secular institutions, is a divine sacred mission, historically indivisible from the other, which is its leaven and fermentation. Humanity also possesses a supernatural vocation which

stems directly from God's plan in the redemption. It aims at placing the Christian ferment in the human mission. It aims explicitly at
ensuring the presence of Christ, his life and his message, in souls and
institutions. It seeks above all to reveal and develop the sources of
this presence: interior, supernatural and sacramental, liturgical and
hierarchical.

But in practice, this double mission that I have tried to differenti-
ate is one and indivisible in the Christian—in Christian society; and
even in society that is simply human and is called to become Christian. This fact must be taken into account above all in the field of education: any Christian education which disregards its human, secular
mission, is in danger of being ineffectual, ill-adapted to its task in the
world and disincarnate; similarly, any human education is in danger
of being falsified, warped and truncated, if it is not imbued with the
Christian spirit. The same goes for missionary action which cannot
afford to neglect all the divine elements existing in non-Christian cultures and religions, but which by relating them to doctrine and calling
on human co-operation is enriched by these new aspects which had
not previously been discovered or assimilated. This promotes mutual
understanding, destroys prejudice and opposition and opens the way
to the Spirit of truth and love.

In determining the authority on which the mission depends, and
the manner of its dependence, it is important to distinguish between
the two aspects of the mission.

When all is said and done, the human mission is dependent on
God. This is obvious. But in everyday life it depends directly on
humanity, who is guided by God and enlightened by their conscience.
The human person is responsible for it: the father or mother of the
family, the worker, the scholar, the technician, the manufacturer, the
trade-union leader, the citisen, and the state authorities.

The Christian mission depends directly on Christ, and on his
Church which continues his work. In his public and private life, the
Christian carries it out under his or her own responsibility without
involving that of religious authority, which does however retain the
right and the duty to enlighten and sanction his conduct. This is the
same for all of humanity, individually or collectively, in private or
public life.

The human mission, however, is not exclusively the domain of the
human person and the secular community. The Church must also

interest herself in it, because often Christian morality is involved. She does this especially in the field of education, social action and charitable works, either by herself or through Christians who are individually or collectively mandated as religious authority sees fit. She most certainly can and must judge and direct the human activities of Christians from the moral and spiritual point of view.

Can every human mission, seen in the perspective of God's plan and animated by his grace, in so far as it answers God's call to extend his kingdom in and through creation, be called an apostolate? Can one talk in this way about the apostolate of the doctor, who carries out his medical practice in a disinterested way, or about the apostolate of the scholar, the father and mother of a family, the manufacturer and the worker, the statesperson?

I have always believed that one can. I have repeated over and over again, for forty years, that this apostolate is essential, irreplaceable, of prime importance. Of course, its degree of apostolic value will depend on each individual conscience. And it is obvious that the light and the help of grace play a leading part here. 'And how are they to believe in him of whom they have never heard? And how are they to hear without a preacher? . . . . But I ask, have they not heard? Indeed they have; for their voice has gone out to all the earth, and their words to the ends of the world' (Rom 10:15–18). But it is often a mystery, and for this reason, who can set up to judge it? How can this grace, which comes from Christ alone, find its way into the souls of all of humanity into an individual soul? This mystery must be at once respected and marveled at, discovered and trusted. And the movements of the lay apostolate, far from disregarding this mystery, ought to fold in it their primary sphere to survey and work in.

The total Christian mission of each person must be called an apostolate. This is the distinctive characteristic of the Christian: each person has received and accepted the life of Christ, and this life is a mission. Thus, their total life is at the service of Christ himself; especially in those aspects which touch the human person exclusively: that is, the human persons' personal, social, professional and temporal vocation. In every true Christian the human and Christian mission is one and indivisible; although its activities stem from a twofold authority, they are in the person totally, entirely apostolic.

The human mission certainly does not absorb the whole of the Christian's apostolate. Moreover, the person cannot fulfil it in this spirit without being connected with and rooted in the sources and all the other vital elements which the person can only find in the Church and in the ecclesiastical forms of the apostolate.

It is, among others, in the ecclesiastical and parish communities that the very sources of their apostolate are to be found, and they must draw their nourishment from them, striving to become an apostle among the rest of humanity around them and even among non-Christians. In this basic Christian community, the parish, people will participate, as far as the duties of their state of life permit them, in the common apostolate of all the members of the Mystical Body, strengthening by their zeal and fervour the apostolic and missionary dynamism of the Church, which must be the leaven of the world.

But to me it seems timely, in fact urgent, to insist today on the apostolic value of the human mission of each lay Christian. It is to this field above all that laypeople must bring their witness and manifest their sanctity. Too often they have had an inferiority complex which has handicapped them on the purely secular level: scientific, technical, professional, cultural, political, national and international. For this reason, collaboration between believers and non-believers sometimes seems difficult, but it is precisely in the secular field that they can and must meet and that laypeople can most authentically be witnesses and apostles.

I believe that I can state positively that any negligence in the apostolic fulfilment of the human mission today entails the gravest dangers. For it is in this field, to a large extent, that the future of humanity is at stake.

6
The World Today and the Lay Apostolate[13]

The world of today! Everyone—scientists, businesspeople, states-persons, the clergy, the pope himself—agrees that this world is, to quote Godefroid Kurth, at 'a crucial turning-point in its history': we are present at the birth of a new world. This new world needs a new apostolate. New, not only in its source and in the contents of its message, but an apostolate made incarnate in this new world, cut out to its proportions, adapted to its scale, meeting its needs and problems.

In order to throw some light on this new world in which we live, and to discover the importance of the historical hour in which humanity finds itself, here are several signposts pointing to its situation.

---

13. In this chapter I shall consider in dynamic perspective the role of lay Christians faced by modern problems, in whose context they must incarnate the living spirit of Christ.

　　The text covers the essential points of a lecture given in 1951 at the opening of the first World Congress of the Lay Apostolate in Rome. It has been brought up to date with regard to its concrete facts (statistics, etc.) and transposed from a spoken into a written style. Since that time we have seen sputniks, interplanetary rockets and cosmonauts; the Berlin wall has been erected; just independence has been granted to a series of young nations; Brigitte Bardot, the transistor radio, Telstar, have appeared on the scene.

　　But these events, and many others, do not contradict the points I have made in my lecture. On the contrary, the problems today (or at least some of them) are considered here in their total, world-wide dimension. But it must not be forgotten that they are felt just as acutely every day and on a personal level by millions of human beings who experience these problems personally. This means that every Christian must face up to and cope with them individually—for his or herself and with their brothers and sisters—to find solutions which will meet both the vital aspirations of all people and the message of the Gospel.

Demographic Factors

The population of the world was estimated:

in 1700 at 623,000,000
in 1800 at 906,000,000
in 1900 at 1,608,000,000
in 1956 at 2,686,000,000[14]

Today it is estimated at about three billion. During the course of the last 260 years it has therefore more than quadrupled. It will reach six billion around the year 2000.

Several centuries ago, the average longevity of the world's population was established at between twenty and thirty years—nearer twenty than thirty—because of stillbirths, infant mortality and the epidemics and periodic famines that decimated the population. Today it is established at less than forty for two-thirds of the world. The struggle against these various scourges has already raised this average in certain countries to sixty or even seventy. If the campaigns for better hygiene, better housing and better nourishment are extended to the total present population of the world, this average will not only be quadrupled (as the figures already quoted show), but multiplied by more than ten, because the average longevity will be three times as long.

These two facts regarding the increase and the longevity of the population, and the means recommended to promote or control them, entail a series of problems of primary importance: problems of person and collective hygiene, the problem of the control and limitation of births, problems of distribution of population, the problem of the distribution of food, commodities, clothing, building materials, housing, etc.

Not many centuries ago, illiteracy was almost universal. In certain continents and among certain races, more than seventy-five per cent of the men and eighty per cent of the women are still illiterate—that is, more than half the world. But in other countries no more than one in ten thousand are illiterate.

In a number of years, the struggle against illiteracy which is on the agenda of the great international institutions, may transform the

---

14. From *Bilan du monde*, Vol I (Paris: Casterman, 1958).

cultural aspect of the population of the globe. What will be the consequences for Christianity, for the Church?

In 1962, the principal religions dividing the world's population are approximately as follows:

486 million Catholics, of whom 67 million are under the Communist regime

456 million non-Catholic Christians, of whom 80 million are under the Communist regime

1,776 million non-Christians, of whom:

300 million are Buddhists

320 million are Hindus

365 million are Moslems

12 million are Israelites

292 million are Animists

392 million are Confucians

95 million are without religion

All these figures must be broken down and redistributed according to countries, races, languages and continents in order to show more exactly the features of the demographic face of the earth. To understand the full apostolic and missionary implications, we need only think for an instant that these figures represent so many immortal souls: *each one* with an eternal destiny, *each one* redeemed by the Blood of Christ, *each one* the image and likeness of God, sacred and inviolable, called to a divine sonship, a divine collaboration, a divine, unique, irrevocable heritage.

And although we live in the most missionary hour of the Church's history, and the hour of her greatest missionary progress, this progress is largely surpassed by the continual increase of the population of the pagan world. During the years between 1925 and 1950, while the population of the world increased by 700 million, the number of Catholics only increased by thirteen million. Thus we can say that for each pagan who is converted every year, more than fifty are born into paganism.

These figures do not point to a final stage of development. The demographic situation is not static, immobile, stationary, fixed. On the contrary, we are faced with a seething world. We are at a new starting point.

Scientific, Economic and Ideological Factors

In order to understand the life and movement of the demographic face of the world, we must take into account the development of the scientific, technical, economic, political and, above all, the ideological factors which are changing and shaping the world at every instant. Never before in its history has it known such lightning upheavals, such rapid, extensive, profound changes.

The mechanisation of work, the power of technology today affect not only the production, transportation and distribution of material wealth; they are also felt in scientific research, in the diffusion and application of | science, culture and ideology. This applies not only to a minority, but to the whole of the human race. People talk about technical humanism, even about the totalitarianism of technology.

The mechanisation of agriculture, the increase in production and exchange involve physical, economic, social and cultural transformations of countries and of entire continents. With scarcely any period of transition or preparation, they abruptly transplant whole populations whose customs and habits could not be more primitive, into highly advanced economic, financial and political regimes. Powerful hydro-electric plants capture and spread almost unlimited sources of energy; vast irrigation schemes transform desert regions into agricultural and pasture land; mining exploration, gigantic enterprises, the transport and intermingling of populations, communication lines by earth and air: all these bring cities and their vast networks of built-up areas into being and it is here that the human masses concentrate. All these economic changes are in the process not only of transforming the face of the earth, but, for the greater part of humanity, the face of life itself.

Entertainment, public opinion, customs and morality, are being increasingly influenced, if not monopolised, by such powerful mechanised means as the plane, car, bus, radio, cinema, television, the press, publicity. To these we can add tourism, sports and the theatre. They exercise a tyrannical influence over the ideas, habits, morality, tastes and aspirations of the masses abandoned to their slogans and their advertisements.[15] Mass-media, those loudspeakers of modern

---

15. 'People talk about a new industry and a new business, which are moreover, very lucrative: "the creation of public opinion" which others call "the falsification of public opinion". (Pius XII at the Jubille Concrress of the YCW, 3 September 1950.

civilisation, penetrate everywhere, into families, schools, transport, work, public and private life.

Preventative and curative medicine, under the influence of scientific and technical trends, creates institutions of hygiene, of social security, of culture, which spread and popularise new modes of living, new ideas of the family, morality and well-being (affecting the transmission, limitation and suppression of life). They ignore and often deny any spiritual authority and finality which claims to transcend and regulate human forces and earthly existence.

All these transformations are staggering and bewildering in their rapidity alone, but they are even more so in the inequalities of their effects. Thanks to these changes, some countries and races are particularly favoured by a constant improvement in their standard of living; but others, the greater part, continue to vegetate in a state which justly deserves to be called 'under-develop'.

On the other hand, within the same nation these sudden transformations have created or accentuated enormous gaps between the social strata of the population itself and between the small minority of the privileged classes and the vast mass of the desperately poor, who continue to live in sub-human conditions. The contrast between the comfort and luxury which are flaunted in the face of unheard of misery is so flagrant and so revolting that it heaps up opposition, hatred and bitterness between classes as between races. What an abuse and perversion of human progress this is!

The devastation of the two World Wars, with their material and human losses, their ghastly practices of race extermination and displacements of populations which are unprecedented in history— (people talk about the 'thousands upon millions' in material losses, the millions of people who were killed, wounded, maimed, displaced or ruined)—has developed nationalistic, racial and colonial distrust and exclusivism to extremes and inflamed the desire for revenge and restitution.

The direction these transformations will take, the multiplication, distribution and use of new products, create problems of responsibility, morality and social justice, and above all, problems of the education and formation needed to measure up to the transformations themselves. In order to be seen in its true dimensions, the problem of responsibility and education would need to be dealt with extensively on its own. The vast scope and importance of this problem can only be fully understood when one realises that there are at present one thousand million young people on earth between the ages of fourteen and twenty-five who are in their formative years, more than half of whom are already at work.

The staggering changes that have come about in our time are not only universal but *unifying*; this is the distinctive character of the time in which we live, and it will have the greatest human and apostolic consequences. Not only will this reach and transform all people and the whole earth, it will increasingly unite and unify the whole of humanity and creation.

Progress in production, transportation, transmission of knowledge and action, not only breaks down distances, separation and barriers of ignorance between people, it also rules out the possibility of people living and producing in isolation from others. The moment that a group of people or a nation want to develop themselves without taking others into account, this logically results in their working against the others. Progress has made people and their actions, existence and institutions so interdependent that the misfortune or ill-will of one becomes a threat to them all, and the aspirations and progress of one a stimulus to them all. A war, a strike, an epidemic, a catastrophe, a discovery, an important ideological movement, necessarily pose problems for the whole of humanity; this is what happened in the case of the oil conflict in Iran, the advent of Communism in China, the working of uranium mines, the discovery of atomic energy, etc.

Today the unification of the world is not only a technical fact, but something humanity is conscious of. All nations, and above all their leaders, know it, feel it, and take it into account. It shows itself in campaigns for the unity of Europe, congresses for world peace, conferences on the colour question; in institutions, meetings, conventions, international and world-wide unions and coalitions, and not only in the public and political, military, economic and financial fields but in all the fields of thought, action and human life. This is the fundamental significance of the Charter of the Rights of Man, UNESCO's programs of basic education, the Atlantic Pact, etc. We only need to go through the agendas of UNO, UNESCO, the European Movement, the Bandung Conference, the neutral governments and all the international organisations to be informed of the problem not only of one country, continent, race, culture, sex or class, but of the problem of all humanity and the modern world.

It is in the world of work and of the workers, as in the focus of a lens or as in a nuclear cell, that this transformation and unification of the world, with its extreme repercussions in the field of thought and life, seems to concentrate its tendencies and the effects it is most likely to have in the future. These effects are firstly, solidarity and interdependence in such things as methods, environment, conditions and systems of work and production. Secondly, and far more important, awareness of and will for solidarity and interdependence in the world of the workers who live and work in areas which are becoming increasingly more compact and explosive', and whose numbers must inevitably grow.[16]

The birth and development of the mechanisation of work has created an enormous class of wage earners in the world, and a worldwide consciousness of the proletariat. This has come about because the spread of this system, caused by prevailing *laissez-faire* liberalism and materialism, has been accompanied by untold misery, injustice and oppression, not only at its inception but right up to the present day, where it is established in countries and among races which are in the process of development.

This is why its worthy, just, humane and universal solution appears as the essential, central condition of a peaceful and harmonious order. In short, if we are to humanise the world we must humanise the world of work.

The solution to the problem of the world proletariat does not solely or even primarily lie in administrative reform. It is firstly—and this is the condition of everything else—a question of humanisation; a question of education, training, organisation and human responsibility which permit and ensure the dignity, the development and the respect of every person, every family and the immense majority of the human race. It must be remembered that this problem of work does not arise solely during working hours in the actual surroundings of work; it has repercussions in the whole of life. Work conditions life.

---

16. The more progress is made, the more it can be affirmed that the phenomenon of proletarisation that is taking place among industrial workers has extended to many other categories: agricultural workers are increasingly a case in point.

'The working-class condition' is no idle term. The human person does not live to work, but works to live.[17]

I only want to refer in passing to the importance of the problem of working-class youth in the world: every year fifty million young boys and girls—half of whom have been to school, and the other half of whom are still deprived of elementary education—enter the environment of work for the first time, far from their parents, their teachers and their priest, and this, at the very age when their personality, their moral, social and civil sense, are being formed; 600 million young people (between fourteen and twenty-five) are preparing to found working- class families which tomorrow will take their place, with millions of others, among the mass of workers.[18]

Worker problem, world problem, human problem apostolic and missionary problem 1

All the problems I have mentioned are today increasingly surpassing the strength and capabilities of individuals and even of smaller communities. New planning projects, more and more numerous and advanced, are being undertaken. They involve the outlay of enormous capital, the distribution of contracts and raw materials, the direction and utilisation of scientific research, and even the systematic organisation of education and hygiene among the people.

The urgent measures which have been taken, or must still be taken to resolve such problems favour the development of bureaucracy, anonymity, state control and totalitarianism. Already the discovery and extension of powerful methods of information and mass culture— radio, cinema, television, press—have brought nearer the danger of automatism, depersonalisation, conform- ism, neutralism, and 'robotism'. People talk about 'brain washing' with good reason.

Only the diffusion of a doctrine, an education and an organisation of society which respect the human person and family, human conscience and responsibility, can maintain and develop in the world a personalism which guarantees dignity and liberty.

We are thus at the heart of the drama. This world in process of unification is a divided world. The methods of thought and action which should tend towards and ensure unity, oppose each other, contend-

17. This was Simone Weil's obsession. Who could ever forget her true-to-life descriptions of the dehumanisation of factory work?
18. The importance of this problem has been strongly emphasised by Pius XII in his speech at the Second Congress of the Lay Apostolate, 5 October 1957.

ing with a totalitarianism which is more and more intransigent. This dualism, this struggle, threaten the peace and even the very existence of the human race. The spectre of an ever imminent aggression drives nations to astronomic expenditure and increasingly prolonged military service. Sensational declarations are made to the public about the manufacture of quantities of weapons and the accumulation of means of destruction which are daily becoming more lethal. If one calculated what the fear of aggression alone and the efforts undertaken to prevent it were costing the world today, one would be terrified. If the same expenditure and efforts could be devoted to abolishing misery, insanitary housing, deficiencies in food, hygiene, teaching and basic education, we could put an end to most of the causes of the struggles between classes and races.

Because of this fear of aggression, whole continents are transformed in an infernal cycle into immense concentration camps which, like gigantic whirlpools, threaten to engulf humanity in a final catastrophe. Fear and panic have invaded the world. The struggle no longer seems to be limited to objectives which can be controlled and foreseen; it has become messianic, redemptive, aiming at the salvation of the world through the victory of force and violence.

More than ever, each human being, each member of humanity, is asking himself the fundamental questions: 'Is the world still fit to live in? Where is it going? Has it any meaning? Who am I? Why do I exist? What does life mean? Does man have a mission? Are there rights and duties? Who is finally responsible? Is there a creative and redemptive God? Is there a life after death, which is at the same time a light and a law before death?'

To these questions, there are some who claim to give an answer, and this not by reason of faith, not by recognising the spiritual forces and eternal truths which rule the material world. They claim that there is only one solution: dictatorship and domination which alone can bring about the triumph of justice and peace and ensure the salvation of humanity. Others fear the time of the Apocalypse, and advocate the politics of the ostrich in flight and despair . . . For them, the world is an absurdity.

As Pope Pius XII stated so precisely: 'Almost all of present day humanity is divided into two opposing camps, for or against Christ. It courts the greatest dangers : the result will be either the salvation of Christ or appalling ruin.'1

The world is at the crossroads.

This is the fundamental problem: can man, can humanity, live without God?

I have only been able to outline a rapid, panoramic and fragmentary view of the human problems in the world of today. This must be the starting point for subsequent investigations and researches, and matter for unceasing thought.

Some could see in it a cry of alarm. For me it is both this, and, above all, a cry of faith and hope. For the discovery of the world's problems is above all an appeal to everyone, priests and laypeople. This the most missionary hour in the history of the Church, this hour in which the missionary field is most extensive and profound, may also be the hour in which dedicated laypeople—growing increasingly more numerous, capable, generous and holy—work to spread the kingdom of God. 'The harvest is plentiful, but the labourers are few; pray therefore the Lord of the harvest to send out labourers into his harvest'(Matt 9:37–38.)

For us Christians, this present historic moment, which will decide the future of humanity, is the moment in which the Providential plan enters into a decisive stage, as much in the order of creation as in the order of redemption. But in a spirit of faith we must be able to see the bond between the problems and the principles, between the facts and the doctrines that were outlined in the preceding chapter; it will not be superfluous to recall these briefly.

Thanks to scientific progress, the unification of humanity is, in effect, a response to the Creator s plan of love. For God has made humanity one, in his image and likeness. He has entrusted to man the stewardship of the earth and the exploitation of all its forces, in order that these may proclaim his glory and serve more and more to make humanity participate in God's life and God's kingdom on earth as in heaven, and in time as well as in eternity.

Today the progress of science and technology, far from opposing this reign of love and glory, enable God's message to be carried to all peoples and to the ends of the earth, and ensure the realisation of this message. The opposition to it which is developing in the world is the increasingly tragic repercussion of man s sin—the refusal to accept God's plan of love. In a tangled network of reactions which are growing more and more confused, all miseries, sufferings and misunderstandings are the logical outcome of the errors, passions and abuses which threaten to engulf the world and humanity in a new deluge of fire and blood. And perhaps for the first time in history all humanity, including men and women of the greatest knowledge and vision, realises in fear and trembling the power of death and destruction to which the abuse of science and omnipotent technology can give birth, if humanity loses the sense of God, of faith, of eternity.

It is in this double perspective—on the one hand the Creator's plan of love, and on the other the terrifying consequences of sin—that the message of salvation brought by the divine Redeemer is proclaimed. It resounds like the prophetic voice of old Simeon: 'For mine eyes have seen thy salvation, which thou hast prepared in the presence of all peoples' (Luke 2:30–31).

Hence it is clear that the unification of the world is above all the time for the development of the lay apostolate to the scale of this new world.

These are the changes and transformations which were mentioned earlier:

— the staggering increase in populations, especially in pagan populations;
— the lightning developments of science, technology and culture;
— the accessibility of new forms of production, well-being and culture to the masses;
— the abrupt and rapid transition to different forms of civilisation;
— the phenomena of mass production, depersonalisation and automatism;
— unification, in the face of antagonism and internal and totalitarian dualism;

All these upheavals and transformations take place on the secular level of life, in the institutions and in the environment of the lay world. It is for laypeople to develop the vast potentialities inherent in these transformations, and to overcome the dangers and obstacles that attend them. Through them the layperson has come of age. The layperson is totally and immediately responsible in his or her personal, family, professional, social, cultural and civic life, both on the national and international plane. For a Christian, these responsibilities are apostolic and missionary, irreplaceably their own.

Hence the urgent need for Christian presence and action which must inspire the evolution of the temporal world. The present evolution demands:

— Christians whose faith is virile, enlightened, formed and tried; who belong to Jesus Christ and live their Christianity intensely, who consciously live his Gospel and his message in the whole of their personal life, with all its secular demands;
— Christians who are conscious of an explicit mission, who know that they are called to work for the extension of God's reign;
— Christians who are present in all the sectors, aspects and institutions of the modern world as witnesses of Christ, carrying the doctrine of the Church, informed of and formed for their lay, social, scientific, cultural, educative mission;
— Christians who understand the importance of forming apostolic communities and of having an organised apostolate.

The Voice of the Popes

It would be a very illuminating answer to the reproach of obscurantism sometimes levelled at the Church to point out that, since Leo XIII (and we could even go back to Pius IX and Gregory XVI), all the Popes who have been present at the birth of the machine age, technology and science, have never ceased to proclaim how the Church could and would help in the development of the world and preserve it from the cataclysms which errors and abuses would inevitably cause. If the Popes have denounced these errors and abuses, it is not in order to condemn science and progress, but to forewarn humanity, and to ensure their ultimate fulfilment for the total good of mankind.

One of the most moving and insistent appeals of the Holy Fathers during the last 150 years was that addressed to all Christians, of all ages and environments, to live their faith and realise their own practical, concrete mission in the heart of the Church and the world and to collaborate with all the progress of the natural as well as of the supernatural order, for the extension of the Kingdom of God. This is the call to the apostolate.

It would be highly instructive to show how the voice of the Popes and bishops has awakened and guided this apostolate of the laity in the Church to the measure of a world which is growing increasingly more complex and fascinating.

The messages, encyclicals, letters, and addresses of Pope Pius XII are in themselves alone illuminating insights and sources of energy in all the fields of thought and action, science and technology and modern life and activity.

The call to the lay apostolate, individual and organised, in all fields, is neither an opportunist solution nor a manifestation of clericalism, fear or panic. It is no other than a call to the essential and total mission of the Church, a call which historic and providential circumstances make so urgent and necessary. The whole concept of the Church is involved, and even the whole concept of man and of the Christian.

This question will be considered at length in the following chapter.

It would certainly not misrepresent the thought of Pope Pius XII to apply to the whole lay apostolate the words he addressed to me in a signed letter concerning the YCW and the apostolate of young workers in the environment of work.

The lay apostolate has 'come into its own, in the providential plan, to help resolve a problem which is not peculiar to a single region or a single continent, the problem which confronts the Christian conscience today: the destiny of so many people threatened in the most precious of all their possessions: faith in God, supernatural life and the eternal salvation of their souls.

The conditions of the modern world, at this decisive turning point in its history, today demand more urgently than ever an apostolate of the laity.

It is only too clear that in a transformation of the world like that which is being brought about in our time, the whole of humanity is being called to assume responsibilities which it has never known in the past. And it is no less clear that many of its members, seduced by a false ideal of human redemption, claim to find the only solution to the agonising problems of the world in the false ideologies of materialism. It is not through taking up a purely defensive stand, a negative attitude, against false prophets that these problems can be resolved, but through the active presence of pioneers who are fully conscious of their double vocation—Christian and human—who are bent on assuming their total responsibility and who will know no peace or respite until they have transformed the environments of their life according to the demands of the Gospel. It is through this positive constructive work that the Church will ex- tend her life-giving action to those souls for whom she has such fervent and maternal solicitude. It is in this sublime task that all apostolically formed Christians are called to share.

7

Dimensions of the Lay Apostolate[19]

Christ is the divine apostle, the divine messenger, the divine teacher and missionary sent by the Father to call all people to participate in his loving plan.

Christ is God truly present in history and in the world, in and through his Son. He is the Way; he is also the Truth and the Life, God for us and with us.

The Church is the mystery of God's communication to humanity, and of humanity's community and communion in God. Founded, authorised and directed by Christ, the leaven and ferment of each new generation of humanity, she carries the person of Christ and his grace, doctrine and salvation, into time and space. She is the mystery of 'Christ prolonged'.[20] Christ's power and authority have been entrusted to the hierarchy in the Church so that it may guarantee in its midst the presence and action of its divine Founder. The hierarchy is the head of the Church. Without it, there is no Church, no eucharistic presence of Christ, no delegation and transmission of authority, and no action of Christ in the Church itself and in the world. But it is not the hierarchy alone, it is the *whole Church*—the whole of the Mystical Body, the continuation of Christ's work, God-made-man, both visible and invisible, which must carry out and achieve its divine mission.

And so it is through the Church and in the Church that God invites all people to collaborate in the apostolate of Christ, the unique apostle.

---

19. The content of this chapter was drafted in its initial form in November 1951, in a duplicated article entitled 'The lay apostolate'.
20. The question of the Church's mission is developed more fully in chapter 7.

When God calls a person into being, when God creates that person in God's own image and likeness, God gives that person a vocation, an apostolate.

Christ's invitation, 'Come and follow me' is meant for every person; *this* is their divine vocation, through the very act of the creation and the redemption. And this is God's plan. The human person isn't simply dependent on God in the natural order; the human person is also dependent on God in the supernatural order, the order of grace, because the human person has been redeemed by Christ. This is why, in God's eternal, unchangeable purpose, the Christian vocation, both human and divine, is universal. We need only follow the continuous revelation of this purpose in the Bible and in the whole history of Christianity and humanity to be aware of this.

'All people are naturally Christian', said one of the Fathers of the Church. This call is irrevocable. Not everyone hears it clearly, but all people are personally called by God, *all without exception*. God's first appeal to Adam and Eve in the garden of Eden—'Be fruitful and multiply and fill the earth', so that the whole of creation should sing God's love and glory—has been not revoked but consecrated by Christ himself.

Today, as it was in the beginning, God's plan of love —creation and redemption—remains one and indivisible. There are not two separate orders: one of nature and the other of grace; there is only one providential order, in which the order of creation is taken up into the order of redemption. Nature becomes supernaturalised. Science, technology, culture and social structures should all serve as means to the redemption. Nothing prevents us from studying the natural laws, whether they be physical, biological, psychical, economic, financial or sociological, but they must be used *for* humanity and not against humanity. And used for the whole human person, body and soul. It is not so much a matter of adding an extra spiritual dimension to the world, as of spiritualising and sanctifying the material universe through the power of grace working in man s whole soul and intellect. God's first appeal to humanity, his invitation to the apostolate, is passed on to us today by the Church, to which Christ entrusted his creative and redemptive mission. And each human being, through the grace of baptism, becomes a participant in it.

If we can say that every aspect of human life concerns the Christian, then it follows a *fortiori* that nothing which bears on the life and mission of the Church is outside his concern.

Everything to do with the specifically religious life of the Church: the life of grace, the sacraments and the liturgy—her teaching on the Bible, the catechism, dogma and Church history—missionary activities and charitable institutions—ecumenical affairs—parish, diocesan and ecclesiastical life—the cares and directives of the hierarchy and its special concerns—the number of priestly vocations—the growth of religious orders and the contemplative life—all these aspects of religious life, and many others as well, affect laypeople and demand their co-operation. For laypeople too are the Church, since they are the People of God. And for this very reason they should have *the sense of the Church*, they must live its life suffer its difficulties and its weaknesses and bear the burden of its toil; they must spread the Church understand it and defend it, and all this at the cost of the greatest sacrifices, even, if necessary, at the cost of life itself.

Although all of humanity participates in the total apostolate of the Church, there are certain aspects, certain fields of action, and certain kinds of apostolate that are peculiar to laypeople alone. This is what Pius XI had in mind when he spoke, in *Quadragesimo Anno*, of 'the first and immediate apostles'. It is these areas of activity which determine what I should like to call the content proper to the lay apostolate, or, as an archbishop put it in more precise terms: 'the specifically lay apostolate of the laity.'

It does no matter what category we put it in; be it Catholic action or social action, individual or organised initiatives, this 'specifically lay apostolate' must act on life itself, and this is where no one can take the place of the layperson whom God, according to his providential plan, has put in a certain place, at a certain precise point in his continuous creation.

The apostolate of the layperson, specifically as a layperson, is therefore that of their daily life, of their ordinary environment, as regards all the problems and responsibilities this life creates, both for themselves and for those closest to them, for whom they bear a responsibility.

It is only when the layperson's day to day life with its particular responsibilities is analysed in detail, that one can have a concrete idea of the nature of their lay apostolate and its richness and fruitfulness.

Daily life, with all its actions and duties, becomes truly apostolic, and this applies to all people alike—the peasant, the worker, the business-person, the scholar, the teacher, the politician, the prisoner and the unemployed; it applies to husband, wife, engaged couples, father and mother, brother and sister, son and daughter; it applies equally to young people and adults, the most learned and the most ignorant the humblest and the greatest. Their lives take on a new value and mean-ing, an apostolic significance which enriches the Church and saves the world. It has been called 'the apostolate of people who haven't got time'; people who have consecrated their whole lives, on every level—be it family, social, economic, civic, scientific or artistic—to spreading and bearing witness to their Christianity.

This apostolate is fundamental; in fact I should say it is the basic, the normal apostolate of every layperson. Other apostolic forms or activities can be added to it, but without it they run the risk of being ineffectual or even compromising. Take the head of a company, for instance: if they do not fulfil their own apostolate in their capacity as the boss, as far as their obligations in technical competence, the practice of social justice, and respect for the person of the worker are concerned—even if they gives thousands for a Catholic univer-sity, for schools, missions, or the building of churches and charitable institutions—they compromise the Church instead of spreading its influence. The same applies to a mother of a family who neglects her husband and children; no outside apostolic group she may take part in will ever replace her own family apostolate. If a doctor neglects their patients, they are hardly bearing an authentic Christian witness to them as a healing apostle.

We need only consider everything that makes up human life to understand the fundamental, essential importance of this apostolate. In fact, it is of prime importance; the absolute necessity of its pres-ence in and contact with all environments and institutions cannot be over-estimated, because it is this apostolate which gives human life its divine value, its supreme and final meaning. It is the founda-tion of all the rights and duties of the human person, it impresses its sacred, inviolable character on him. It is the basis of all morality and sanctity. And it is in this apostolate that the Mystical Body of Christ—its life, its apostolicity, its influence and its mission—finds its fullest expression and realisation. The more the layperson's apostolate is understood, the more widely it is spread, the more the Church will grow in sanctity, and the more she will become the spiritual ferment leavening the dough and restoring the whole of creation to God.

The layperson must rediscover God's mission in the secular life of humanity, and link it with the mystery of the creation and the redemption. Both in and through life—work, science, technology, education, international action—the layperson must bring back to the secular world its divine, sacred, redemptive meaning. This is the whole *consecratio mundi* that Pius XII has spoken about so often.[21] The Church's first missionary task is to help all people towards this discovery: 'Go and teach all nations' (Matt 18:19).

There is sometimes a tendency in certain circles to separate temporal and spiritual life, or else to set them against each other. If we do make a distinction between them, it should only be in order to show the unity that exists between them.

Life on all levels—family, social, scientific, cultural, civic and political—in short, the whole of lay life—has secular and religious aspects. They should not be confused, but neither should they be separated. This would be laicism.

Now, more than ever, religious life cannot afford to ignore secular life. If the various problems of humanity are to be properly studied and resolved, this supposes one basic approach to human nature and human destiny, which are inseparable. The solutions that are being proposed and put into action today by the great international institutions, make it still more imperative for Christians to concern themselves with these questions, with a view to the whole future of humanity and religion. Competence and sanctity, far from being mutually exclusive, should always be integrated. We need saints who are doctors, workers, and business people, social and political leaders, parents, husbands and wives, if we want to hallow God's name in every sphere of human activity.

The layperson's spiritual life, moreover, is not only expressed through the worship of the Church, the liturgy and the sacraments; from these indispensable sources it wells up in the very heart of the humblest lay life which places itself increasingly at the service of God.

Some people are still averse to using expressions like 'the social doctrine of the Church' and 'Catholic social action' because they have

---

21. *Inter alia*, in his speech at the Second Lay Apostolate Congress in Rome, 5 October 1957, and the speech to the YCW World Conference in the same year.

certain clerical implications and suggest an outmoded concept of Christendom. Obviously much less attention should be paid to the words used than to the facts; but we should give the reality behind these expressions the true meaning and value they deserve. The Church does possess a doctrine about humanity, the family, work, and the system of work. If she cannot have or formally propose specific techniques which will implement these doctrines, she is nevertheless, obliged to express her disapproval of in! human techniques which make this incarnation impossible. It is for her to inspire, raise up and promote human structures which remain human and can be sanctified. The essential bond between temporal and spiritual life reveals the interdependence between the one and the other, between matter and spirit, time and eternity.

We are well aware of how much environment, technical development and governmental systems influence man's life, his morals and his ideas, and *vice versa*. This bond is not purely natural, it is supernatural and doctrinal as well. It does not rule out the necessary distinctions and autonomies, for example, between Church and state, religious responsibilities and human responsibilities (family, professional, scientific, etc), nor is it opposed to any kind of venture, research or civilisation; it inspires, consecrates and purifies them.

We must acknowledge without embarrassment or prejudice that even in the promotion of purely temporal human progress—technical, social and cultural—the Church and the apostolate have a role to play, an efficiency that the experience of centuries serves to make ever more obvious. That there are and have been abuses for which Christians and even Church dignitaries have been responsible, that there have been religious prejudices, no authority of the Church will deny. The error, in this domain as in all the others is, unfortunately, due to our fallen nature, and it is only through the efforts of all people—believers and non-believers—that it can be combated and checked.

At all events, today more than ever, lay Catholics, precisely because they are lay and Catholic, must be in the foreground of all secular initiatives; they must increasingly develop their human competence and capability in order to have an impact on the religious plane as well as on the secular.

The invitation to the apostolate is meant for all laypeople, for all men and women of every age, social condition and environment, and for all human activities, whether temporal or spiritual. This invitation is implicit, but it becomes explicit to the extent that the individual becomes conscious of it, discovers the bond linking him or her to the Church, the hierarchy, Christ and God, and has recourse to the sources of grace which are essential to the apostolate.

Little by little the person comes to see it as a way of life, a whole spiritual conception of life: in a word, as their personal vocation. Experience proves—and I will never stop repeating this—that the discovery of the apostolic dimension of daily life produces incredible results in the simplest Christian lives: both in the radical transformation of environments and as an irresistible impetus towards personal perfection. Far from cramping or crushing the human personality, this apostolic conception of life is a powerful motivating force which finds its expression everywhere, in the most neutral fields, for instance m scientific and artistic circles, sports groups, amongst old-age pensioners . . . In short, it is an individual apostolate.

In the strict sense of the word, the lay apostolate is the collective, organised apostolate of laypeople. I would need a whole chapter to deal with it in all its aspects: its aim, its importance, its organisation, its services, its formative and representative action, and its method's of evangelisation and penetration; all this needs to be more fully and deeply developed on the basis of recent experiences.

All lay apostolate organisations, whether social, cultural or professional, no matter what sphere of activity or aspect of lay life they deal with, are proving increasingly necessary as problems become more important. Have we thought enough about the place we must give to the apostolate in the world of work, of leisure and culture, of mass media and public opinion? What a vast number of investigations have to be carried out concerning vocational guidance, automation, the unemployment of young people and adults, travelling and migration, the life of the big cities, the rural world and its relation to the industrial world, ecumenism and the lay apostolate, missionary problems and interracial relations. And think of what the lay apostolate can do in international fields! For this it needs to be still more competent, it needs a more extensive network for collecting data, an organisational complex always more closely fitted to the need, and speedier, more concerted and efficient possibilities of influence and intervention. Wherever there is a sphere of the modern world where the future of humanity seems more in jeopardy than elsewhere, and where the layperson's role is more decisive, that should become a key position of the apostolate.

The lay apostolate, organised in the secular field, is always and everywhere the answer to the call from God and the call from the world, in all the problems, old and new—nova et vetera—which never-endingly rear their heads and influence the destiny of a humanity growing dimensions of the lay apostolate 103 tually more numerous, more organised and more highly developed.

Catholic Action is a more official form of the lay apostolate; it is mandated, and involves the hierarchy more directly. Up till now, in practice, it has been organised and carried out above all among young people. Obviously, it is of prime importance to them. Like every apostolic movement, it is the indispensable complement to educational instruction and formation; you could say it was the field where training and teaching are finally put into practice in real life, and where they bear their first Christian and apostolic fruits.

What is more, the problem of young people today—and the YCW has had experience of this with the young workers—is an international problem which extends to all races, and which all the big institutions are trying to resolve. This is where apostolic organisations must bring the youth of every country in the world into action, and to do this they themselves must be organised on an international scale, while respecting the prerogatives of the diocesan and national hierarchy.

The fact that apostolic movements up to the present day are principally being put into action by young people, does not lessen the importance of, and the urgent need for an apostolate among adults; unless such an apostolate exists, all the efforts of the young people will lead to a dead-end. We must acknowledge that since the Second World War a serious effort has been made to promote this actively, and where adults have really taken it seriously, it has given rise to the highest expectations. Obviously, the nature of adult commitment will differ from that of young people, and the diversity of temporal commitments in particular will set plenty of apostolic problems.

'You will renew the face of the earth.'

This is the eternal problem set by the very mission of the Church: the nature of her presence in the world.

Forever unchanging, yet forever new, the Church must continually adapt to cope with the conditions, the problems and the new dimensions of humanity. She is essentially apostolic, not only in the head of her visible hierarchy, but in all her organs and members which are deeply rooted in life and which must take part in resolving human problems and transforming the world.

This is the problem of incarnation which requires that the Church must assimilate the world into itself while leading it towards its ultimate fulfilment. In this ascent of humanity, in which the hierarchy points the way and provides spiritual food, the lay apostolate, working in the world, is building the city of all people which must also be the city of God; it is transforming the earth into a better dwelling place, so that the People of God, always growing more numerous and more united, may be able to carry out their earthly mission there and achieve their eternal destiny. While the face of the earth is being transformed, humanity must become sanctified by the presence and actions of those carriers of light, those witnesses and pioneers—the lay apostles. Head and members, closely united to Christ, and through Christ united to each other, will penetrate new structures, purify new discoveries, be present at new conquests, and hasten the coming of the Kingdom of God.

If the Church is not present in the world through her head and members, humanity will founder; the most magnificent discoveries, instead of enriching and promoting the progress of the world, will threaten to engulf it in homicidal struggles, errors and abuses, even in universal catastrophe. The further forward humanity goes, the more it needs the total apostolate of the Church. More and more, the leaven must work in the paste. The sources of grace must increasingly nourish all the members, reaching to the very confines of the body of the Church, so that these may finally attain the confines of the earth and absorb the whole of humanity. All apostles must be convinced of the true dimensions of the problem; they must have a sense of their participation in the Church's mission, so that the world may see the divine, bountiful and redemptive presence of God manifested in humanity.

Only in the measure in which the local church, united to the world-wide church, carries out the unique apostolic mission of the head and the members will darkness be vanquished by light, error by truth, hate by love, and evil by good.

It is in this measure that the infinite, eternal glory of God will be revealed in time and space; that all creatures of the natural order—the fruits of technology, new institutions and structures, cultures and civilisations—will sing the glory of God, their Creator and Redeemer, their beginning and their final end.

From this we must infer that all the value of the Church must be given to the lay apostolate, without which the spiritualisation and divinisation of every aspect of human life cannot be effected. The layperson must see and understand his own responsibility, and everything possible must be done to involve and sustain him in the effective realisation of his duty in the life of the world. This responsibility will grow greater in the future.

People talk about 'the hour of the laity'. Surely this day in which we are living is that hour, the time of technical competence and responsibility, as well as the time of apostolic formation and responsibility? What we are advocating is not Manichaeism or Pelagianism, but total Christianity.

Everyday experience has made us well aware that an apostolate orientated in this way will stir up a whole series of questions and concrete problems: What is the layperson's apostolic responsibility towards the temporal aspects of life? Is the layperson's presence in the Church arid in the world a responsibility of the Church? How far is the layperson dependent in his apostolate, and how far is he autonomous? What methods of organisation are most suited to the development of an adult apostolate? How can the ecclesiastical character of these methods be reconciled with the incarnation that must be carried out in secular spheres? Each of these questions, and many others, must be carefully studied, while taking into account doctrine, experience, and particular needs. The answers will doubtless involve many differences of opinion, but they should never lose sight of the fact that the lay apostolate is a way of life which grows unceasingly while adapting itself to the human condition. This growth cannot be hindered or paralysed by ready-made solutions or abstract discussions.

'To restore all things in Christ'. St Paul's command is certainly relevant today! We are no longer concerned with the Roman, pagan world of his time. We have before us today a world in which humanity has been bound in economic, technical, sociological and political ties, and which is awaiting the time when the cultures and communities of mankind will become more closely united. Will this drive towards unity result in internal struggles and antagonisms which will lead to collective suicide, or will it become a source of mutual aid and understanding, a source of confidence for the elevation and salvation of all people and for the establishment of a truly fraternal commu-

nity? This union of humanity and the world, in accordance with God
s plan of love, can only be redemptive and beneficial under the ban-
ner and the inspiration of Christ.

While all the false messiahs are confined to time and will end in
annihilation, the only true messianic movement, Christianity, opens
time into eternity and leads humanity towards its only end—the living God.

This is the only answer to the deepest aspirations and anxieties
experienced by man in every age.

Some time ago, an economist surveyed the economic and technical history of the last fifty years under the striking tide 'The Civilisation of 1960'.[22] While his account sticks to realities, it is also full of
optimism. He doesn't make the slightest reference to spiritual forces
or even to Christian virtues, but he ends his book with a very telling
reflexion:

> From now on, however, we feel certain that the near future
> will witness the union of all the conditions necessary for the
> intellectual culture of the masses. The average man will regain
> the time which has been at his disposal during the preceding
> ages, but which he has lost in the period of transition, to
> think about the one real problem in the world—that which
> the theologians call the problem of the last ends, and which is
> really the problem of life itself.

This one basic problem, which some people have claimed to brush
aside, remains today in the face of all the possible errors and abuses
of science and atomic weapons: 'Why do I exist? Why do I live? Why
do I work, and think, and love? Why was I born, and why must I die?'
These are the fundamental questions humanity is asking itself today,
questions that can only be truly answered by faith; which completely
permeates life, which becomes the whole act of life. This is the only
peaceful victory that can give the answer to these questions. The lay
apostolate, which is vital, living faith, which has been put to the test,
must make it shine in every field of life, so that it may be 'the true light
that enlightens every man coming into the world' (John 1:9).

---

22. Jean Fourastié: *La Civilisation de 1960*, Ed. Presses Universitaires du France,
Collection 'Que Sais-Je?' Paris 1950.

Part Three
Will The Church of Tomorrow
Have an Authentic Lay
Apostolate?

8

Priests and Laypeople in the Church's Mission[23]

In returning to one of the most important points of the lay apostolate, which was only barely outlined in the preceding chapter, I am not merely repeating myself; I want to develop more fully this vital question of the Church's mission, and this includes the mission of the layperson. Considered in the light of the Church's mission, the layperson's mission can be seen from another angle, from which we can infer new facts and conclusions.[24]

The whole of the conversion and the sanctification of the world comes about through Christ, according to his doctrine and under his leadership and guidance. In order that the mission which he began should be continued, Christ sends other people who carry it out in mystical union with him, as the body is united to the head; 'Abide in me, and I in you' (John 15:4). 'And lo, I am with you always, to the close of the age' (Matt 28:20). This mystic union with Christ, this body of Christ, is his Church, and it is in loving unity with her that Christ wishes to complete his mission. She is the *Sponsa Christi*, the bride to whom he has entrusted the realisation of his ideal She is the *Corpus Christi*, his body in which he continues his task and remains present on earth, teaching sanctifying and generating his life.

---

23. A lecture was given on the main points of this and the following chapter at a Priests' Study Session in the Breda diocese of the Netherlands in January 1951, and later published in the Session's pamphlet report, under the title *Arbeidersjeugd in de Zending van de Kerk*.

24. Although this book is meant as much for laypeople as for priests, lay people will give me leave to speak more particularly to priests in many of the passages in the following chapters. Hence the frequent use of 'we', in which I am identifying myself with the rest of the clergy.

We receive the person, the grace and the mission of Christ in the Church, and for this reason she is also our mother, *Mater Nostra*, because everything we have comes from her and through her. And so the mission of the Church, like the mission of Christ, is to restore the whole of humanity to God and to put the whole of creation back into the plan of divine love. '*Instaurare omnia in Christo*—to unite all things in Christ; things in heaven, and things on earth' (Eph 1:10).

The Church, too, must be the leaven of the world, the light of the world, the salt of the earth. She must transform humanity, reveal the true way to all people and make her grace available to them, so that the whole world may participate in the work of redemption through the complete collaboration to which it is called. 'Go therefore, and make disciples of all nations' (Matt 28:19).

But we must never forget that this is the mission of the entire Church, and because the whole of the Church must be holy, it is the whole of title Church too which must be orientated towards the realisation and the extension of the work of redemption: *the whole Church must therefore be apostolic.*

Priests and laypeople together make up the Church. It is together that they must carry out Christ's mission. The Church is not a democratic institution. Her mission is not decided by the faithful, who designate authority or give her a mandate, nor is it the faithful who lead her, but Christ: the Church receives her mission from him and through him alone. He it is who determines the task, who gives the orders, the power and the authority. And so the Church is hierarchical, vested with sacred power and entrusted with a divine mission.

It is here that we see what the real mission of the hierarchy is. The pope and the bishops are those who are called *by* Christ, mandated, ordained and vested with power in order to represent Christ and direct the faithful towards God's loving design. They are mandated *for* the Church, for the faithful and for all people: 'for every high priest chosen from among the faithful is appointed to act on behalf of the faithful in relation to God . . .' (Heb. 5:1).

The hierarchy, then, must ensure the presence of the person of Christ and establish the community of man with God, so that humanity may thus be restored to him; 'to act on behalf of the faithful in relation to God, to offer gifts and sacrifices for sins' (Heb 5:1).

Consequently, there is *nothing* in the Church which can exist or come into being *without* the hierarchy. If the Church only exists through Christ, she cannot exist without his representatives, the bishops, and their delegates, the priests. *The hierarchy makes the Church into the Church of Christ.* It was through Christ alone that the ultimate union of humanity with God was realised; through its head the Church has become the Mystical Body of Christ and takes part in the Saviour's mission. And so it is through the hierarchy that the Church receives from Christ the mission of saving the world.

The whole Church is incorporated in this mission. And by the whole Church, I mean priests and laypeople together.

To think that the priest alone plays an active role in the Church and that the Catholic layperson is only a passive listener and recipient is to have a mistaken notion of the hierarchical order. The layperson, too, in the common mission of the Church has an active task to accomplish, his own responsibility to assume, and the priest, called by God, but mandated for man, must develop an awareness of this responsibility in the Catholic layperson. We shall see later how the priest does this, and what the nature of the responsibility is.

On the other hand, the layperson must receive the person, the life and the doctrine of Christ, so that, growing in grace and making Christ truly incarnate in their own life, they may carry this divine life not only within their own soul, but to all their brothers and sisters: at work, in their social capacity, in their environment, and in any institutions where they can exercise their influence or give witness to their Christianity.

Pope Pius XI once said to me, with a smile: 'I write encyclicals, and I'm very glad to do it, but it's impossible for me to transmit all that they contain to the workshops and factories, because I'm just not there I The onus to do this is on the laypeople who work there . . . Neither bishops nor priests can do it because they aren't in these environments . . .'[25]

The people who are actually living and working in the ordinary circumstances of everyday life are the laypeople, and it is up to them to carry out Christ's mission in all the different temporal sectors of life and to make the whole Church present there. I can never repeat this often enough: the lay apostolate is irreplaceable.

---

25. . It is impossible to deal with the question of worker-priest here: this matter needs to be considered at length and a good deal of research is necessary.

In relation to the lay apostolate, the hierarchy must assume its own task, which has various aspects and is put into action through priests who are delegated to work on all the levels and in all the activities of the life of the Church.

First of all, the priest must reveal God's plan to the faithful and make them aware of the place they occupy in it. In other words, it is the priest's duty to bring each Christian to a discovery of their true mission, and, through teaching the Good News, to throw light on all those errors which beset the layperson on every side: false missions, false doctrines, false messiahs.

The priest must reveal this message not only to those who have been baptised, but to all people. He must be especially concerned with those who are not baptised, and who are not yet part of the flock: 'And I have other sheep, that are not of this fold; I must bring them also' (John 10:16). The Church is for all people, she belongs to everyone. And because of this, she must have apostles and preachers. 'But how are people to call upon him in whom they have not believed? And how are they to believe in him of whom they have never heard? And how are they to hear, without a preacher?' (Rom 10:14).

Above all, the priest must communicate the person of Christ to the faithful, for without Christ and his grace, without union with Christ, the layperson cannot achieve his or her mission. The sacraments were instituted to this end; they exist for people. The priest is the 'pontifex', establishing the bridge between God and humanity.

But it isn't enough merely to reveal their mission to laypeople The priest must go further; he must stir in them a desire for the apostolate, he must help, encourage and guide them in their understanding. Every priest does his utmost to increase the number of priestly or religious vocations; but shouldn't he also obtain lay apostles for the Church, and a great number at that? Shouldn't he also be the founder and promoter of the lay apostolate in his parish? He should want to make apostles of all his parishioners, looking continually for men, women and young people who are noble and generous enough to dedicate themselves wholeheartedly to the cause of Christ and the Church.

For this, the priest must know his sheep, and the parishioners must know their shepherd.

And finally, these lay apostles must be formed. This is a task of capital importance which will be dealt with at length later. It is, to a high degree, a priestly task, of which Christ himself set us an admirable example, even down to the practical details, in his patient training of the twelve disciples.

This task is to communicate faith to the world, to sanctify and christianise the life of the world in all its dimensions. Laypeople must truly be the light of the world and the salt of the earth, for it is only when they become the real witnesses of Jesus Christ that the Church can animate the whole of human society with the spirit of Christianity.

And so they must open themselves to the sanctifying action of God and develop a personal spirituality which will give them strength to carry out their mission in its fullest and deepest sense. It is only then that they will be capable of truly fulfilling the apostolic command.

If their apostolic mission is centred essentially in their environment, with its temporal institutions, they have to bear their personal responsibilities on two levels-— human and Christian. They must develop a profound sense of this responsibility, as well as the qualities which needed to put it into action: human capabilities, brotherly love, a vision of the world and of the Church, audacity, courage, perseverance. A great many Socialists, Communists, and other militants who set up human messianic movements are to be admired for their consciousness of responsibility, their strong will and their steadfastness and toughness in action. Every Christian inspired by the spirit of love should be inspired by this radiant, dynamic force. In actual fact, how many of our parishioners and Christians are still a true light to the world?

We must acknowledge that the layperson's own role in the sanctification of everyday life is still unknown to many people, and it is exactly for this reason that the priest's awakening, educating action is absolutely vital. Priests must tell laypeople over and over again, they must convince them that their own human life is the field of their real and specific apostolic vocation.

It is true that a certain number of laypeople have already responded to the Church's appeal, which has been addressed to them more specifically during the last decades. We can even ask ourselves from time to time whether the roles haven't been reversed: isn't it sometimes a case of laypeople, already aware, trained and committed, trying to pass on their conviction to priests, so that they too will discover the place of the lay apostolate in the apostolic mission of the Church?

I will not go back in detail to what I said very explicitly in Chapter Two. The following notes are only a reminder, to help stress the priestly action in the formation of an authentic lay apostolate.

— Each layperson, whatever their function in life and however modest their capacities, has in their own life and environment an apostolic vocation which they alone can fulfil; in this their mission is absolutely personal.
— It is also irreplaceable, in the sense that if they do not fulfil it in the circumstances in which God has placed them, the Church will be unable to realise her mission to the full.
— The priest's and the layperson's mission differ from each other not only because of the kind of apostolate they exercise, but because of their fields of action. The layperson's apostolic field is civic, cultural, economic and social life, the family, work—the whole of secular life,
— Because of this the mission of the layperson and the mission of the priest in the Church are complementary. The priestly apostolate is not complete because the priest is not living in the very centre of temporal life, and he cannot transform and sanctify it from the outside.
— Because the layperson alone can influence the environments of secular life from within, their apostolic mission is indispensable. This isn't an amateur's job. Where would the Church be, for instance, without work and without the sanctification that comes from work and through it? Where would the Church be without completely christianised families?
— The layperson's apostolic mission belongs to the very essence of the Church, whose task it is to further the work of Christ.
— Each individual layperson must be a witness and an apostle of Christ and the Church. This is why they bear the name of Christian: 'The Christian is another Christ!' This name carries dynamic meaning.
— The layperson must not, however, be a witness separated from otther Christians. Only together with the other Christians of their community, together in the movements of an organised lay apostolate, can they contribute most effectively to the Kingdom of God.

— Finally, the apostolate of Catholic Action is an official mission, mandated and organised by the hierarchy. In practice, the movement is adapted to the big sectors and essential functions of life, and especially to social environments, to age and sex, using appropriate methods and other means of expression as the case may be.

Today [the early 1960s] there are about three thousand million people on earth, some five hundred million of whom are Catholics. This means, if we dare admit it, that we live in a world where the greater part of mankind does not know or will not recognise Christ, that we live in a non-Christian world, or, as some people say, in a 'post-Christian' world, whose conceptions, judgments and way of life are not guided by Christian principles.

Formerly, the problem was not the same. From the quantitative point of view Christians were only a minority, but it was possible to maintain clearly defined Christian centres and to preserve a Christian mentality there. Through sheer lack of contact the pagan or anti-Christian spirit didn't influence Christians in the same Way as it does today. But now we live at a time when all sections of mankind can inter-communicate with incredible ease. Formerly, when distance was a barrier to communication, people did not know what was going on in other places; but today the entire world seems within our reach. Everything that happened during the Korean War the exploits of Gargarin and John Glenn, the course of events leading to the independence of the Congo or Ghana, the main forces at the Twenty-second Congress of the Communist Party in the USSR, the events of the Vatican Council: all these are known to us and everyone else, even in the smallest village.

Each person, and therefore each Christian, is like a fortress that is constantly being besieged and battered from all sides. Through a thousand different visions of life, through all kinds of events, incidents and atmospheres, regimes, systems and ideologies, he is in continual contact with error.

In the face of all these systems and currents of thought, whatever they may be, there is only one complete, positive answer: Christianity. But it can only mean something if all the members of the Church fully and worthily accomplish their mission.

Let us consider first of all the influence of this modern phenomenon on the inner life of the Church herself.

If the faithful are not fully aware as Christians, if they do not have strong personal convictions, they will never withstand the onslaught. How could we be content with a Church most of whose members were prompted by a purely passive docility?

This sheep-like mentality, this lack of personally based conviction, is almost certainly the reason why so many lose interest in the Church and then fall away. They will fulfil their religious obligations as long as they are living in a carefully protected environment, but as soon as they leave this conditioned environment, a great number of them will abandon the practice of their religion and finally the faith itself.

Now, it is impossible to steer them clear of every danger, or to arm them beforehand against every evil influence. The Church is not a ghetto, set apart from the outside world, which preserves her members from its influence. We live among other people, and all people are free! But there is also the other aspect: the needs of this outside world. The Church must reach out to all people and penetrate the whole of life. She must be present in all environments and in all institutions, even the most secular; she must penetrate international institutions.

If laypeople do not have an apostolic spirit, the Church will be driven out of secular life, both public and private. She will no longer reach all those who are either ignorant of her or oppose her; she will lose all influence on the development of world events; she will no longer be able to pour out the spirit of Christ on every creature. If she no longer has the means of fulfilling her mission in its entirety through the presence and intervention of laypeople, which nothing can replace, we are moving towards a total dechristianisation of life, towards a world which increasingly turns away from God.

Only a living, active Christianity, therefore, can meet this twofold threat and build a Church that is truly according to Christ's will. In the achievement of this active Christianity, priests and laypeople have a common mission but different functions. Working together they form one in the realisation of the Kingdom of God.

9
Priests and Laypeople Working as a Team

'Apart from me you can do nothing . . .' (John 15:5)

The meaning of these words of Christ, reported by St John, is perfectly clear to us: there can be no apostolate, either priestly or lay, without Christ himself, the only apostle. We must apply this saying to the indispensable role played by the priesthood in its dealings with the lay apostolate. There can be no lay apostolate, whether individual or corporate, without the apostolate of the priest. There can be no other apostolic channel, because he alone can give Christ to the people. It must be added at once, however, that without the lay apostolate, the priestly apostolate is powerless to carry out the human, Christian transformation of the world. The union and the reciprocal collaboration between priests and laypeople is therefore essential to the unity of the Church and her mission, and to the fulfilment of every apostolate. This collaboration is essential, whatever the immediate objective of the lay apostolate may be:

a. temporal and secular: laypeople must discover and realise the divine, apostolic and missionary value of their actual lives in all its aspects (family, work, leisure, economic security, participation in civic life national and international relations etc.)
b. ecclesiastical: catechism, the liturgy, the sacraments, parish life, diocesan or super-diocesan life etc.

With regard to the first, we might say that priests are the priestly collaborators with the lay aspostolate; in the second, that laypeople are the collaborators with the priestly apostolate. In both cases, the priesthood is at the heart of the lay apostolate. The priest has a magnificent, sublime function: it is he who must inspire, raise up, guide, nourish

79

and sustain the apostolate of the faithful. And this through his entire priestly ministry; not as a side line or an accessory to his ministry, or as a hobby, luxury or extra, but as a necessity and essential.

This is the only true, full conception of the priestly apostolate.

I have had this thrilling experience myself, and I have seen it realised by many priests.

The administration of the sacraments, the celebration of Holy Mass, preaching, preparation for the profession of faith, the cate-chism, prayer and the recitation of the breviary, visits to families and the sick, all the parish activities and movements: these are so many sources, so many ways and opportunities of raising up and sustain-ing the lay apostolate. Its apostolic significance must be continually emphasised by the parish clergy.

When I was a curate, I did more in the confessional to stir and stimulate the lay apostolate in the parish than by any other means, and I am not afraid to admit it!

The parish community, which is the Church present and immedi-ate, on the spot, is an essentially apostolic and missionary institution. And this applies today more than ever everywhere and in all circum-stances. The pastor with all the clergy, is its head. The parishioners, families and organisations of the parish are its members

The parish community is like a great team, based on a number of small, specialised teams which, dovetailing into each other and complementing and supporting each other, all reaching out towards one and the same goal: the establishment of God's Kingdom among all people.

The priestly team is formed by the parish clergy. If there are two or more priests in a parish, it's easy: their team is ready-made. If the priest is by himself, he must join up with other parish priests and curates in neighbouring parishes. Together they must unite, pray, pool their resources, teach, inform, and support each other with regard to their apostolic work; together they must build up the Church where they find it, survey the field to be worked, study the problems that arise, and be on the alert for the echoes that reach them from the environ-ments of work, culture and leisure.

They must unite themselves with the apostolic movements of other parishes, of the diocese, the whole Church, the country and the world. They must enlighten each other about their experiences.

They are 'in the apostolic movement'. And they are its promoters: the head, the heart, the soul, the motivating, uplifting force.

Vae solil—Woe to him who is alone! This is as true for the priest as it is for the layperson. Alone and isolated he is powerless.

If it is a proven fact that the layperson's mission belongs to the very essence of the Church, that priests and laypeople each have their own mission in the whole mission of Christ and the Church, and that these are complementary to each other, then the combined team of priests and laypeople is a logical requirement.

As I have said over and over again, teamwork is essential in the Church as a means of complementing and completing mutual aid. Only on this condition can Church fulfil her total mission.

The priests who make up a team among themselves must also unite with the leaders, militants, organisers and all responsible for the lay apostolate. Priests together with laity form the militant, dynamic Church.

They must have meetings with laypeople and keep in touch with them so that they may come to know and understand their life and all their temporal difficulties, problems, environments and institutions. In this way they can also follow the militants in the fulfilment of their daily apostolate, whether this be in families and districts, or far from the parish, in trains or buses, in the places of work, in moments of relaxation and in the places where they spend their spare time. It is often through them that priests become aware of the vastness of the problem of evangelisation, by getting to know the number of those who remain outside the traditional life of the Church, and the reasons for this state of affairs which has been brought about both by the present development of the world and by the irresponsibility and deficiencies of Christians themselves. Through them, too, the Church becomes actively missionary, the parish becomes a 'front line' parish, reaching out to all those places where the parish itself, the Church and Christ are not known, are attacked, or are thwarted by the pervasive forces of materialism and militant atheism. For it is here, where laypeople live and act, that the lost sheep are to be found who must be brought back to the fold; scatter the sheep. 'The laypeople', said Pius XII in a famous speech,[26] 'are in the front line of the Church's life'.

---

26. At a secret Consistory on 18 February 1946.

These teams where priests and laypeople work together are a source of mutual enrichment and give rise to exchanges of experience and information. You have to participate in them to realise, with a conviction that daily grows stronger, that they offer inexhaustible possibilities of hope and spiritual resources. In these teams, there is a whole strategy to be continually learned, renewed, adapted and extended.

How true, too, is another remark of the same Pope: 'In decisive battles, the most successful actions sometimes start from the front, and here the history of the Church offers plentiful examples.'[27]

Lay apostolate movements and the parish

I am not concerned with setting the first against the second, or vice-versa. I started the YCW in the very heart of parish activity, and I have always wanted it to be on a parish basis.[28] But this does not exclude the essential vision of an apostolate which goes beyond parishes, with the organisation and activities that would be the normal consequence of this. Far from it. Neither does it exclude apostolic groups which have been formed to meet specific needs without first having taken root in the parish (e.g. groups acting in technical schools, youth clubs, big industrial units, etc.)

Far from being at loggerheads, far from interfering and clashing with each other, the parish and the movements of the lay apostolate are, for me, inseparable and divisible. The parish will always be the cradle both individual and corporate work in the lay apostolate: it is there that the apostolate is born and nourished. It is there that it takes its place in the Church. Both looking steadfastly to the one final goal, the parish and apostolic movements cannot be alien or external to each other. They are essentially 'one' in the Church and in Christ. All the frictions and difficulties that arise can never be resolved by opposing them to each other, or by ignoring or rejecting one or the other. Apostolic organisations and the parish not only complete each other outside, in an apostolic field far distant from the parish; they reinforce each other within, in the very life of the parish which then develops the whole stature of its mission. Experience proves this.

---

27. Speech at the first Congress of the Lay Apostolate in Rome, 7 October 1951.
28. The first pamphlet I wrote for *Editions Jocistes* in 1925 was called: *The YCW and the Parish*.

If the lay apostolic movement goes beyond the confines of the parish or even the diocese, or the country, and sends laypeople out to the world (and this would indeed meet the needs of our time) it can never be at the expense of the parish or the diocese. But here we need an exact conception and a missionary vision of the parish in the Church.

Of course I have said often enough that the lay apostolate is a world-wide problem. But the world which is to be transformed and saved is not to be found outside the parish; it starts there, it becomes incarnate and takes roots there. In spite of appearances, the destiny of the World is, in a sense, decided in each parish, and every priest is responsible for it. Pius XI never ceased proclaiming: 'Their destiny is in your hands . . .' (Ps 30:16): the destiny of the faithful, the destiny of the Church, even the destiny of the world.

Can we still really distinguish a Christian land from a missionary country? Paganism is everywhere, and the entire Church has become—or reverted to—a missionary Church. Each parish is, and must be, a missionary parish. Because it is in each parish here, as well as beyond the seas in some Asiatic or African country, that the problem has to be faced. This is why it must be solved on the spot, at the root of things. And in the measure in which it is solved at its base, it will already to a great extent be solved for the world. We must not forget that lay apostles must come to us from parishes: this is where the christianisation of the world begins and grows and comes to influence and pervade the whole of humanity. If we priests, in our priestly work, have this constant concern, we need not fear for the future.

The unity towards which the world is moving at the present time is not so much, nor solely, a danger to the Church and Christianity. It also contains a very great promise. After all, have we not the whole of creation at our disposal? The possibilities have never been greater, we have never had so many rich and numerous occasions of bringing Christ to all people, thanks to the techniques which can and must be put at the service of the Divine Message.

Do not believe that the times in which we are living are only difficult and full of worry or anxiety. We should rejoice because we are living through the finest pages of the Church's history: at the present time she is moving towards her total dimension, not only geographically, but through the action of all her faithful. For never in her history have we seen laypeople so aware of the needs of the Church and of their brothers, never have they been so conscious of their mission and so ready to fulfil it, with a faith and charity that are particularly dynamic.

And all this amongst the lowliest and the weakest. What ' us things have been achieved, for instance, by the young missionaries of the YCW!

The layperson will never understand and realise their mission unless they have a living faith. In this the priest must serve as the example.

The priest who wants to inspire and raise up vocations to the lay apostolate must first of all have great faith himself. This condition is essential. If his faith is not alive it will be not only a dead faith, but a faith that kills. We do not have to strain our ears much to hear laypeople telling us why they have lost the faith, and why they have left the Church. 'My righteous one shall live by faith' says St Paul (Heb. 10:38). This is what we have most need of. And we can be sure that laypeople, in their own way, can recognise it when they are talking about priests with whom they have been in contact: 'Oh, Father so-and-*so believes!*'

The priest must be a man of invincible faith. He must firmly believe in God's plan, he must have an unshakable conviction that God desires the salvation of all people without exception: '. . . God our Saviour, who desires all people to be saved . . .' (I Tim 2:4). Yes, God wills this. He will achieve it in time and eternity. The priest must have faith in the victory, he must believe in the death and resurrection of Christ, in the success of his redemptive mission: 'I have overcome the world!' (John 16:33).

In the same logic of God's plan, he must believe in the mission of the laypeople as a means of christianisation which is really willed by God. If we priests do not have confidence in this mission in the heart of the Church and the world, how can we ever apply ourselves to forming them? If we are not fundamentally convinced that the lay apostle can succeed in leading the world to God how can the layperson have confidence in the goal he or she must pursue and in its final outcome?

But if we dare to believe and to appear certain of the victory, laypeople will feel confident that they are capable of doing great things for the Kingdom of God, and will accept their responsibilities in a great spirit of faith: ' . . . this is the victory that overcomes the world: Our faith' (1 John 5:4). And instinctively, I have always added: the faith of the priest.

Naturally, this power of priestly faith is brought to bear on the difficulties inherent in the collaboration between priests and laypeople. We must never hide these difficulties from ourselves. Who would imagine that a task like this—the formation of other Christians to be the collaborators of Christ the Apostle himself—could be easy? In these tribulations the priest must be able to say like Christ, 'And for their sake I consecrate myself, that they also may be consecrated in truth' (John 17:19). Indeed, only the priest who believes in his priestly fatherhood will be able to give his life, his whole life, to save his sheep.

We need only think for a moment about the appeal of the Holy Father Pope Pius XII concerning the workers' apostolate which I have quoted earlier[29] and which can be applied to all the other sectors of the lay apostolate, to understand how vain this appeal is unless there is a corresponding priestly faith.

And finally, the general resolutions of the Second World Congress of the Lay Apostolate must be re-read and meditated on, especially those which relate to the formation of laypeople to their apostolate;[30] and then one will understand the absolute necessity and urgency of the increase of apostolic vocations, especially amongst laypeople, the greatest need of the Church in the present time? I would be tempted to believe so.

Sometimes people are afraid that the new stress placed on lay vocations may be the cause of a diminution of priestly and religious vocations. I don t believe this at all. The apostolic value of work, marriage, the family, the whole of temporal life, cannot be over-emphasised. But we must point out always and to everyone that the sense of this apostolic value cannot be achieved and diffused without priestly and religious vocations which are totally and finally consecrated to awakening and spreading it. How many laypeople, both young people and adults, recognise with touching pride and supernatural love the role that a certain priest or chaplain has played in the orientation of their whole secular life towards the apostolate. On the other hand, how many priestly and religious vocations have been directly inspired and born in the groups of Catholic Action, through an apostolate working concretely in lay life? An objective investigation would clarify this question. Even now, my own personal experience convinces me that

---

29. At the very end of chapter 6.
30. In *Laics dans L'Église*. Published by Comité Permanent des *Congrès International pour L'Apostolat des Laics*. Rome 1958.

the conclusion would be positive: I could give figures and numbers of Witnesses that would prove without any possible doubt how fruitful the lay apostolate is in the multiplication of priestly, religious and even contemplative vocations.

The priest must always and everywhere raise up these vocations, through all the means and opportunities his ministry offers him. So the lay apostolate itself, especially that of the young people, will become a kind of normal apprenticeship for the apostolate of the layperson's whole life and therefore for the priestly and religious apostolate. When we think of the five-sixths of humanity without priests, when we realise that all humanity urgently needs a greater and greater number of people who are dedicated entirely and exclusively to the apostolate in all its forms, it is easy to realise how much every priest should be driven on by the desire to increase lay and priestly apostolic vocations.

Because in the Church today the Virgin Mary has been placed far more in the foreground of Christian piety, laypeople must discover what part she plays in the realisation of the Church's mission, what she means to the Church and to all of us.

Mary is truly our mother and the mother of the whole Church. It is through Mary, the mother of Christ, that we have received him, and through her that the mystery of the redemption of the human race was made possible. Without Mary, there is no Church, no Pope, no bishops, no sacraments, no apostolate . . .

And Mary was not a priest; she was not a nun. She was a lay woman, a young girl, a woman of the people, living simply among the people; she was a mother like other mothers, living in the framework of her country and her time.

Mother of us all, priests and laypeople, Mary is also the example for us all. But now, when the lay apostolate is being advanced, isn't she especially an example for laypeople, in their own irreplaceable mission in the heart of the Church? For in Mary, they discover the necessity of their vocation, the dignity and sanctity of their state.

All of us, priests and laypeople alike, must see in her, fully realised, the collaboration between God and man. Thus, in the perfect gift of herself, she reveals the very aim of all our endeavours.

Together, aspiring simply and courageously towards this goal, we must realise the last words of Christ to his apostles: 'That they may all be one, even as thou, Father, art in me, and I in thee; . . . so that the world may believe that thou hast sent me' (John 17:21).

10
The Formation of Laypeople for Their Apostolate[31]

It is obviously not enough to seek out and raise up apostles. They always have to be trained. I have never found a ready-made militant. What is more, they must be trained 'with what is available', with people as they are; just as we were trained, just as Christ trained his own apostolic companions.

The Church prescribes six years of formation for those who intend to go into the priesthood before sending them into the world to evangelise. Can we be irresponsible enough to think that the layperson can be sent into the world—an indifferent, often hostile, sometimes corrupt and increasingly pagan world—without a deep and solid formation? I am convinced that without this he will find it impossible to face and cope with the situations that he will meet in non-Christian environments.

He needs this a *fortiori* if the Church demands that he transform a paganised world, sanctifying and consecrating it for the glory of God. After all, this is the layperson's explicit mission, and how can we expect him to fulfil it if he is not prepared for it?

In just the same way that there can be no priest without a seminary, no religious without a novitiate, no doctor without a university, and no craftsman without a technical school, there can be no lay apostle without a specific formation. We need a kind of lay seminary whose methods are perfectly adapted to life if we want to make Christians capable of saving the world. I want to make it quite clear that I am not talking about forming specialists in the apostolate, in the sense of 'full-time' leaders, or in the way that UNESCO trains experts

31. This chapter first appeared in a duplicated article, 'L'Apostolat des Laics', November 1951.

in basic education. No, I am talking here about all lay apostles, whoever they may be, who are working quite simply as witnesses in the limited sector of human life in which the Lord has placed them; those who are carrying out in their everyday life what today we usually call the 'basic' apostolate; those of whom people say 'they haven't got the time' and who must learn to transform their whole time into the most fruitful of apostolates.

It is not because people call him, slightly incorrectly and probably for want of another expression, 'the simple layperson', that they can rest content with a too rapid, simple minded, or even superficial or childish formation for him. There must be no cheap Christianity, no so-called popular formation! We must aim at an authentic, thorough, profound, demanding formation for everyone, even the simplest and the least humanly endowed, which while certainly taking into account the methods and adaptations of healthy popularisation, will be centred on the profound work of grace in every soul, intellect and will, which blossoms there into a theological life that cannot be measured in human dimensions.

If we talk about 'the simple layperson' like this, there is all the more reason to apply these considerations to those who bear wider and more specific responsibilities.

Formation must be related to the mission. We must always come back to the starting-point, which is the layperson's actual mission in the Church and in the world if their formation is really to correspond with their needs.

This must never be forgotten and must be repeated time and time again: the mission that belongs to the layperson, because he *is* a person, consists in discovering the secular and divine mission of humanity and linking it with the mystery of the creation and the redemption; he must give the temporal world its divine, religious and redemptive meaning.

There are three paragraphs in Pius XII's last speech to the YCW[32] that are particularly significant in this respect: 'The Church today more than ever needs young workers who will build valiantly, in joy as in affliction, success or trial, a world according to God's will, a fraternal society in which the suffering of the lowliest will be shared and lightened.'

---

32. There are numerous other texts in which Pope Pius XII proclaims and develops the idea of he consecration of the secular world.

— The YCW 'is striving to restore in all its nobility the Christian conception of work, of its dignity and holiness. The actions of the young workers should be thought of as the personal acts of a son of God and a brother of Jesus Christ, through body and spirit, for the service of God and the human community. May this conception of work penetrate factories, offices and professional schools through the members of your movement. This is an apostolate which is essential and practical to a very high degree.'

— 'You are Catholics in the fullest sense of the word, that is to say, not only as individuals professing the truths revealed by Christ and living personally by the grace of the redemption, but as members of the Christian community, fulfilling your own task in this community, a task which is indispensable to its life and its equilibrium'

From this we can see immediately that the layperson is living continually and simultaneously on two essential planes of existence: the secular and the religious. Because of this, the formation that the apostolate demands must always refer back and relate to these two planes, distinct from each other, yet indivisible.

During the last four centuries, secularisation and individualism have had too much influence on religious life. This is why lay life, with all its multiple functions, is generally considered something that has nothing to do with religion.

Today, thanks to all kinds of new factors in philosophical and theological thought, in sociology and pastoral |tfe, we are beginning to see that the Chinch and religion cannot remain outside the construction, humanisation and development of the world. While they are distinct from the responsible secular authorities and technical methods of work and progress, the Church and religion cannot be ignored or separated from this evolving world. Such a separation would be fatal for humanity and for the Church.

To separate the religious from the secular when formation for the apostolate is being considered would be even more catastrophic. This must always be taken into account when reading the following pages.

I should be very glad if one day laypeople were to deal extensively with the human, technical and educative aspects of apostolic formation—the questions of human qualifications, fitness for responsibility, adapted methods etc.—and here the experience of the last thirty years could provide rich material for a very useful synthesis But I want to stress at this point the religious, theological, ecclesiastical aspect, or, in short, the authentically Christian aspect of this formation, because it falls directly within the province of the priest.

Laypeople, even though they sometimes appear to show resistance, aspire far more than one realises to a solid, profound formation. Above all they need religious formation; we priests should give them a true concept of supernatural truths. Many adult laypeople, sometimes even intellectuals, have what in fact amounts to a childlike or even childish religious formation. They picture the truths of the faith to themselves in just the same way as they did when, as children, they learned their catechism before making their first communion. With such a formation, it is impossible for the adult, especially nowadays, to stand firm in the face of the countless difficulties he meets in his environment, still less to influence and transform this environment.

In conjunction with religious formation properly so-called, it is obviously essential to give a sound formation to the will, which will put into practice the truths of the faith and all that they imply about life. The teaching of a healthy Christian asceticism which can be suitably embodied in lay life (not an asceticism modelled on that of priests or religious) is absolutely essential in the face of the lax but often seductive atmosphere prevailing in modern life. This asceticism will also be one of the tests of the true value of the faith. But above all, this religious formation and asceticism must imply apostolic formation they must become a powerful stimulus to the apostolate. This formation must teach all people to revere God's name, always and everywhere, to do his will, and at the same time to establish and extend his kingdom. The apostolic value of secular life must be emphasised unceasingly: it is the only answer to all the false messianic movements of our time that continually threaten not only Christians but the whole of mankind. Theological faith and life, deeply incarnate in everyday realities, must be revealed as the only positive, dynamic, victorious answer to secularisation. They can be applied to life in manifold ways: in the apostolic value of work, love,

the family, professional and civic life . . . What driving force, what conviction and pride this conception will inspire in the soul of the simplest and most ordinary Christian!

It is in this way, in its apostolic perspective, that I have always conceived the religious formation of all the faithful. Yes, I mean *all the faithful*: not only the faithful organised in apostolic movements or involved in parish organisations, but all laypeople without exception—the mother of a family, the doctor, the errand boy, the farmer, the invalid . . . . all those who do not have the time or the opportunity to take part in an organised apostolate. In these cases, however, formation cannot be confined to something general, or summed up in Church in the Sunday sermon, which must inevitably be the same for a greater or smaller number of listeners. We must aim at formation which is more specifically adapted to the needs of different categories of the faithful: formation for children, for teenagers, for married couples, intellectuals, workers and peasants, etc. But all this with a single goal in view: to form active Christians lay apostles whose religious life is truly incarnate in the whole of their everyday existence.

For if the Church is always stressing the apostolic collaboration of laypeople, the latter cannot be limited to receiving teaching! It must become effective through action, usually through an apostolic movement. And there is neither action nor movement if we are merely satisfied with giving lessons and lectures.

We must search for entirely appropriate and concrete means of ensuring that the layperson does not remain a passive listener, but learns first of all to think for themselves, to meditate actively on the truths of the faith. This is how laypeople will learn, little by little, to exercise their own apostolate: as mother or father of a family, tradesman, invalid, worker, or peasant . . . The training to be given must be such that it will lead laypeople to act on their own initiative, and this through giving them concrete responsibilities that they will gradually assume by themselves.

To live as true Christians: this is something the priest can never do for them; they must do it by themselves. But the priest must initiate them, encourage them and help them. This is how they will become powerful and effective.

The Christian presence of laypeople in the whole of life and all the problems it sets—whether of science, technology or social and human progress—will demand increasingly deeper and more extensive formation in the future.

But it is absolutely certain that the essential condition, the very soul of the apostolate, will always be its permanent contact with its fundamental sources. No one can give what he does not possess.

There is only one Apostle and one apostolate. The apostolic sources and ends are intimately linked.

I shall attempt to distinguish and discuss several of them further on, but this question needs to be gone into much more thoroughly. For each of the sources of the apostolate I mention, one must look for the concrete implications, the ways in which it is introduced into secular life, the positive and negative experiences relating to it, the results obtained, and the future directions it will take.

The more I think about the importance of forming lay apostles and note the outcome of the ventures of the first years, the more I dream of a World Congress of the Lay Apostolate, where an extensive study can be made on the subject of formation alone, once it has drawn up an inventory of all the needs and problems with which the layperson of today is confronted. How richly we could benefit from this! With this as a starting point, a concrete, dynamic program could then be outlined which would draw up the content of this formation in all its aspects.

The visible signs and links of sanctification, the sacraments, must be explained and experienced as a participation in the apostolate of Christ and the Church. These are not signs that work mechanically, but *living signs*.

Take baptism, for instance: the parents and godparents of the baptised child must understand the meaning and duties that baptism involves; they must make its effects and commitments understood to the child, and be willing to bring him up according to the necessary requirements, so that the graces of baptism may have all their sanctifying effects. It is the same with all the other sacraments that restore or increase sanctifying grace, and provide the graces necessary for a certain state of life—marriage or holy orders—and make such a state of life apostolic.

In the measure in which all the dignity, riches and marvels wrought by the sacraments are translated into living action, they will bring about a dynamic transformation in the whole of life. This is a discovery which can be made time and time again and which can never be obscured by habit or routine.

However, we can see the practical obstacles, raised by economic and social changes, which keep the faithful away from the sacraments. I have always been obsessed by the thought of the thousands of workers who leave their homes before the churches open in the morning and only come back in the evening when they are shut; the law concerning the eucharistic fast, although it has been lightened considerably, is still impracticable for a great number; access to the confessional and the father- confessor is often difficult, not to say practically impossible in certain parishes. It is essential to study the pastoral problems of Christians who are in need of sacramental grace to be true apostles.

Since its foundation, the YCW has faced this fundamental need with attempts to restore living, apostolic meaning to the sacraments through concrete activities: the renewal of the baptismal promises at the end of religious campaigns: participation in the mass by all the young people from one neighbourhood or one place of work; marriage services followed by Mass, Communion and promises of apostolic commitment, etc.

On the Other hand, active participation in all the liturgical ceremonies demands a constant effort. Particularly when they are taking part in Holy Mass, laypeople, both young people and adults, must become more and more acutely aware of one fact: together they form 'a chosen race, a royal priesthood, a holy nation' (1 Peter 2:9). This means that their whole life—their work, their family and social relationships—is a host offered to God rendering glory to his creative power and redemptive love and expressing through Christ adoration and gratitude to him who is the author and the end of all things.

Every apostolate, whatever it may be, derives from and converges towards the sacrifice of Christ which is continued in the eucharistic sacrifice, the centre and climax of the liturgy. Thus, the sacrifice of the Lord assumes the whole of life; the whole of daily life continues the sacrifice, becoming a prolonged mass which makes Christ, priest and victim, present everywhere, sanctifying all things and presenting them to his Father.

Ite, Missa est. When the mass has finished, the layperson must realise that it is this same redemptive mass that impels him to action in the world: 'Go forth now, you, the laypeople; go forth to your mission, to your work which is the sacrifice of Christ continued! Your machine, your work-bench is an altar; and you, the sick and suffering, are nailed to the very cross of Jesus Christ! . . .'

Then the liturgical year becomes the secular year itself; instead of only taking place during religious ceremonies within the walls of the Church, it is realised through family life, at work, in society. And liturgical formation enables people to take part in the highest and most solemn expression of parish life; it is a direct preparation for the Church s worship, a worship which is no longer put on one side of life but which transforms and inspires it.

In liturgical life so understood, it is the Mystical Body which, in a great impetus of faith and charity, deepens its unity in its leader, Christ. It draws its life from the same apostolic spirit, which does not admit any fundamentally separated apostolate—an apostolate of class or an apostolate of race; it is pledged to the apostolate of Christ himself through all its members, and in all the places in which they live, with the sole aim of the glory of the Father.

All the practical means of formation (which no one can afford to despise and which have stood the test of experience among laypeople) find their justification here: the liturgical calendar, the missal, sung or dialogue mass with a personalised offering, paschal campaigns, etc. They are precious aids to a constant renewal of spiritual life.

Sometimes it is even necessary to start with the most elementary kind of initiation. Often, when I was working in a parish, instead of holding meetings with the first young militants, I used to give a living demonstration of the mass: we used to meet in the evening at the Church of Laeken and there, as the boys and girls stood around the altar, I showed them the sacred vessels, explained tiie symbols, and celebrated before them and with them the most significant actions of the eucharistic sacrifice. For most of them it was such an extraordinary revelation—and one that came about in an atmosphere of respect and simplicity—that it was impressed on them for the rest of their lives.

All these means of liturgical formation are a constant reminder of the true end of the apostolate and a caution against any deviation into purely temporal activity. *Sursum corda—Habemus ad Dominium* expresses that action which is continually drawing the hearts of committed Christians towards the heart of Christ.

If their apostolate is to be a living, authentic one, laypeople must learn to know and love Christ more and more in the light of eternity as well as in the temporal perspective. And here we must begin with the historic Christ, the centre of all history and creation. The more the Gospels are understood and meditated on, the more plainly he will emerge through a deeper understanding of the Old and New Testaments, and the more clear and illuminating God's plan for humanity will appear.

The movement back to scriptural sources which is at present taking place amongst Christian people is not the least of the providential coincidences of this century, which takes such eager interest in history and historical sources and interpretations. But there is one condition: these sources must be put within the reach of all laypeople as authentic sources of Christian, apostolic life. The Gospels and the Epistles are not only meant for the Christians of the first centuries, they are meant for the Christians of the twentieth century too. More and more, the clergy need to be in a position to explain them in such a way that they can be adapted to and made incarnate in the world.

Biblical history must be completed by the history of the Church, and even by that of the eastern and western civilisations of the world, so that everyone will become aware of and see in its true light the cultural, scientific and temporal progress that Christianity has brought to humanity. Without refuting anything, neither the merits it has brought, nor the faults it has committed, the historical vision of the Church's presence in the world will reveal better than any theory the value, the efficacious power and the true substance of the lay apostolate.

To a large extent, the mention of the hierarchy evokes instinctively and solely an image of laypeople reduced to passive obedience: people talk about clericalism, unwarranted interference in the temporal domain; they feel paralysed in action or have a sense of inferiority.

The formation that we must give the layperson in this field must help him to discover the grandeur of the original bond between the apostolate and the hierarchy, and consequently, the dependence of the apostolate on the hierarchy. This guarantees authenticity, safety, confidence and victory. Christ is present in and through the hierarchy; its words and doctrines are those of Christ. His grace transmitted through the hierarchy does not transform the baptised into passive instruments or minors under guardianship, but causes them to participate in the privileges and responsibilities of the sons of God, the carriers of the Gospel message.

This is why formation as to the meaning of the hierarchy must be a preparation for a dialogue with religious authority and the clergy. Indeed, thanks to this dialogue, laypeople will understand that hierarchical authority does not act as a sort of extinguisher which aims at clerical control, but that its action is a source of progress, liberation and redemption: 'The Son of Man came not to be served, but to serve . . .' (Matt. 20:28). 'My sheep are known to me . . . the good shepherd lays down his life for his sheep' (John 10:14, 11). In their relations with the hierarchy, laypeople must be brought to discover the Spirit of Christ—the spirit of holiness, light and love— of which the hierarchy is the trustee. It is a spirit of selflessness, dedication and service unto death. The spiritual power with which it is invested is a power of life, respect, justice, charity and peace.

Seen in this light, all apostolic dependence will then become a communion with the life and concerns of the Church. A dialogue which is carried out in faith between religious authority and laypeople engaged in the apostolate is a means to a fuller understanding of the real needs of the world on the one hand, and of the problems facing the Church on the other. Little by little, in loyalty and submission, it will help to find the answers and adaptations with which the Church must meet the greatest problems of current life.

We must realise that we are only just beginning work in this field. But laypeople who have had experience of it feel themselves increasingly to be sons of the Church, responsible for her mission to all people, and are encouraged to accomplish the task which rests with them.

Recourse to all these sources of the apostolate sanctifies the Christian. Through them, he participates in the grace of Christ and consequently in the life of the Trinity. Henceforth, he is no longer left to his own powers and weaknesses, he is invigorated by the power, the light and the love of God.

And through this very fact, these sources also sanctify the life and the world in which the layperson carries out their daily apostolate. It is through the vital impetus of grace that he can build a world that is both more human and in greater conformity with God's plan.

Of course, these divine, supernatural forces with which the layperson is nourished do not suppress or replace the human energies and capabilities—intellectual scientific, social or technical—that the layperson needs to accomplish his task, but they purify, illumine and stimulate them. They can never serve as an excuse for negligence on the professional or human plane; on the contrary they make even greater demands on the layperson. But on the other hand, no natural, human force can ever take the place of the quickening and impetus that spring from supernatural faith and charity.

These must increasingly be sustained and renewed by prayer, meditation, interior life, spiritual direction, retreats and recollections. But these means too will never attain their total dimension unless they are constantly incarnated in life, in the concrete, temporal mission, in all the circumstances of the apostolate. The interior life and the apostolate are as inseparable as the soul and the body.

The whole of secular life is nothing other than the realisation of the Lord's Prayer, the synthesis of all religious life: 'Our Father, who art in heaven, hallowed be thy name, thy kingdom come, thy will be done on earth as it is in heaven.'

What I have been stressing up till now, on every page —the fundamental relationship between life and the apostolate—will probably not surprise anyone. What has been said should perhaps suffice to indicate the essential place taken by secular life in the total theological and practical conception of the apostolate. However, I want to emphasise one last time the central role played in apostolic training by attention to life. If life must be one of the essential bases of a sound theology, it is, at the same time, a methodological base without which we would only be making artificial gestures, aiding and abetting the divorce, of which we are all witnesses, between religion and the world.

I am convinced that to ignore or underestimate in supernatural and apostolic formation the humblest, sometimes the most obviously down-to-earth aspects of life, will always mean a deficiency, often a fault, and sometimes a deformation.

People must be careful not to misinterpret the allusion I made at the beginning of this chapter to a lay seminary'. It goes without saying that I would have no part of a formation that takes place behind closed doors, between the walls of some institution or other, however orientated towards the world its teaching program might be. This seminary must find its fulfilment in everyday reality; not in a room, but outside, in the open air!

There is no need to say that, for me, attention to life means attention to the transformation of life through absolutely essential individual and collective action. We must start with life itself if we want laypeople to transform and consecrate it. And we must look at life objectively if, little by little, we are to replace human vision and judgment with the vision and judgment of God. It is through permanent contact with life that we will strive to transform it, in order to integrate or reintegrate it totally in the divine plan.

This is the method—see, judge, act—that Pope John XXIII was pleased to mention in his encyclical *Mater et Magister* as a means of human and supernatural education that should be used to train laypeople and apostles and authorities. It inspires the total apostolic dialectic that I talked about in the beginning, with a vast vision of faith, hope and charity.

This is a concrete method, realistic and effective. For me, laypeople are not formed for the apostolate through books, purely theoretic teaching, or spoken lectures however magnificent, or even through discussions, although these may be means of rounding off formation in helping to draw up various syntheses. Laypeople are formed first of all by the discovery of facts, followed by a Christian judgment, resulting in the actions they plan, the plans they carry into effect, the responsibilities they shoulder. The method involves the exercise of all the human faculties and at the same time the use of all the supernatural and apostolic resources which have already been considered. And through a constant vision of the needs of all those who must be saved, it is an extraordinarily powerful impetus to progress and personal sanctification. This is a total, vital, existential apprenticeship to the apostolate; it generates an ideal, a way of life, with personal and communal demands corresponding to the huge measure of the apostolic task.

The review of life, already so well-known in the circles of the lay apostolate, is one of the most important aspects of its method: see, judge, act. It is not only an irreplaceable method of education, it is also a precious element in spiritual direction and formation. All the first young militants of the YCW had their own note-book' which was, among other things, a means of entering directly and profoundly into the concrete details of their everyday life; they prepared their visits and their conversations there, in a way which was both practical, stirring and exciting. Whether it is made alone or at a meeting of the team, this review of life is a means to the apprenticeship and fraternal control of the total transformation of everyday life.

So the priest who carries out his educative task loyally, patiently and selflessly, using the method: see, judge, act, possesses the master plan of what could be called 'apostolically based education', on which we can found our finest hopes.

I could cite thousands of facts and countless personal testimonies of people who have literally been trained by this method for a total and final commitment to a mission which has absorbed their whole life.

Such an apprenticeship comes about progressively. I said at the beginning of this chapter that militants are not found ready-made; to start with they must be taken just as they are. But once they have made the discovery, once they have caught on, they are able to fulfil the increasingly greater demands that are specified in a program of life adapted to their human and spiritual possibilities.

It is quite clear that formation carried out in this perspective and according to these methods could never have a purely individual character. There is no need to repeat that the apostolate of each lay-person must be essentially communal, a collaboration with all his 'neighbours'. Even where the elite is concerned, it cannot act apostolically from outside; it must be the leaven of the crowd, working within the crowd itself; it must be the germ of a community, in living communion with all people.

If we sincerely want to entrust laypeople with their total responsibility, if we want to send them out towards the World which awaits them, their formation must obviously be of a social and a communal kind. Today, when all the sectors of life interpenetrate each other, it would be unthinkable to ignore this aspect; such negligence would make laypeople, and more particularly those who are rooted in the working class world, powerless in their everyday environment.

I cannot here sufficiently develop the question of social formation properly so-called: formation for the social doctrine of the Church, for social action, etc. To deal with it in a few brief paragraphs would only minimise it.

I would like rather to insist on the necessity of setting the apostolic life of laypeople in a communal frame-work, illumined by a communal vision. Formation in particular—because it is this that we are dealing with—must be given and put into practice within' the human compass. This formation must certainly always be a personalising one which develops personal conscience and personal resources; it must never neglect any individual apostolate which is not officially organised. But the other dimension, that of a concerted, group apostolate, must never be despised. The problems arising today from life lived in common can only be resolved by an organised apostolate which meets the dimension of these problems. It is in groups within ordinary human life, designed to the measure of the problems to be resolved and the environments to be transformed, through teams of apostolic communities of all kinds, that this apostolic formation is bound to act most efficaciously. There is an infinite variety of possibilities to meet all temperaments, all outlooks, and all the degrees of commitment, from the team of three or four families in the same part of town or belonging to the same profession, to the great national and international movements with religious, professional, cultural, or charitable objectives; the range is immense.

But first of all we must see the sign of a Christian spirit which is also a communal spirit: one cannot bear witness alone, just as one cannot be saved alone. We must also see the need for a true Christian realism, and here in many respects *Mater et Magistra* gives us a magnificent example. It is essential to discover the advantages of common commitment, which permits leaders to help and direct each other as brothers on a completely equal footing. No one will deny the power of education and training that this implies. If the priest is the animator and educator, this is all the more reason for him to remember that laypeople form themselves amongst themselves through brotherly contact with one another and an interaction which permits all individual qualities and responsibilities to be brought into play.

Common commitment is common responsibility for the solutions that are adopted for the problems of life; responsibility towards the particular people for whom one is working; responsibility for the organisation to which one belongs or which one leads. All these aspects must be further deepened, so that all men, priests and laypeople, may discover the extraordinary riches of the lay apostolate movements; and in the process of this deepening we shall probably come to realise that we are still only taking our first faltering steps.

It is in this perspective that the problem of those who are called 'the unorganised' must be studied and resolved. To seek easy solutions for them, which keep them from all commitment and all responsibility, is to condemn them to a social and human inferiority bringing with it the most pernicious consequences. The masses can never be lifted up without leaven; and we will never have enough leaven without a movement which trains and penetrates them.

At present, apostolic commitments carried out in common lead many laypeople to an increasingly conscious desire for perfection, which expresses itself in very different forms of spirituality. These lay gatherings, whether or not they are officially approved by the hierarchy, will always demand a certain stability in spiritual as well as apostolic commitments. Such teams introduce into the very heart of the lay environment aspirations and testimonies of Christian charity, poverty, detachment, purity—in short, a fully Christian life according to the Gospels. Their very presence is an apostolate, a revelation of God to the world, 'good tidings'.

This is on condition, however, that they never form cliques cut off from the world, shut up in' ivory towers which are a pretext for self-satisfied judgments on those who do not share the same outlook; on the contrary, they must be wholeheartedly open to the world and all its needs, inspiring a universal apostolate for and in the masses of Christians and non-Christians, an apostolate which is selfless and loyal. Spiritual groups must never claim the monopoly of carrying the responsibility and the direction of lay apostolate organisations. These conditions, moreover, are equally valid for every apostolic body, every movement, and every organisation in the Church.

It is difficult to say whether all these reflections bear more on lay-people or on priests.

Through their formation, it can happen that priests acquire certain habits of thought which separate them from laypeople. I should demand emphatically that they keep in close touch with ordinary life whether they be chaplains of Catholic Action, teachers, spiritual directors, engaged in the parish clergy, or in charge of retreats. To neglect the everyday life of laypeople, and consequently the true field of their apostolic mission, is often to deform and nearly always to weaken their commitment to the duties inherent in that life in which they have been providentially placed.

It is the duty of the priest to help laypeople to discover the apostolic significance of everyday life and their task in the organisation of the world. It is not for him to lead, but to educate. He can neither take the place of laypeople who are responsible, nor can he impose himself on them. But how can he educate them effectively for the apostolate in life if he is not familiar with lay life and does not try to understand it through listening to laypeople? For he himself does not take part in lay life—he must learn its true problems from laypeople. One is often appalled by the ignorance or lack of awareness of certain priests in the face of these problems; I have so often said this where the problems of young workers are concerned.

Pastoral care that is apostolic in spirit must be enlightened by temporal life.

To many priests, the task of educating lay apostles seems particularly difficult. Many of them are afraid of undertaking it (perhaps because they have a certain unavowed fear of laypeople themselves?); others have started enthusiastically but have been quickly discouraged. These priests must be understood and helped. If I have already strongly stressed the faith which conditions the priest's perseverance—'*usque in finem*—until the end' – I should also add that he must receive an adequate preparation for his role, as must the laypeople. I feel that to claim the contrary would be absurd. If the collaboration between priests and laypeople is to be a powerful source of the apostolate for the whole Church, all priests must be prepared for it. Whether they belong to the diocesan or regular clergy, their formation with a view to the lay apostolate must be an integral part of all preparation for the priesthood, both in the seminary and in theological colleges, a formation which grows increasingly more detailed and profound as they approach the exercise of their ministry. This could include a serious study of the problems which laypeople must resolve in the modern world, in order to work out priestly methods of helping them in their apostolate at the very heart of events and institutions. They must be taught this as an essential part of pastoral work.

This teaching must be sustained by gradual participation, becoming more and more intense, in the apostolic activities of committed laypeople: participation in the study-weeks of leaders and in the life of local groups, contacts and investigations, holiday camps, etc.

This practical knowledge must be increasingly deepened and adapted for those who are called to be chaplains and Church assistants in apostolic organisations; this applies not only to chaplains who have been totally released for the task on a regional, national, or international scale, but also to chaplains among the parish clergy who assume the primary task of the basic formation of leaders. The various types of formation undertaken by priests could be adapted to specific needs and conditions of the environment, and to the methods and techniques appropriate to age, sex, etc.

However we must guard against splitting the clergy into those who on the one hand are working for Catholic Action and who specialise in collaboration with laypeople in apostolic organisations, and, on the other hand, the parochial or teaching clergy. All the clergy must be formed for the lay apostolate because this must increasingly be seen by everybody to be an apostolate of the Church, forming an integral and inalienable part of the Church's mission.

Nuns, too, will more and more be called upon to collaborate with the lay apostolate, some in teaching institutions, others in medical or charitable work, parish activities, etc. A certain number could even be called to be counsellors within the girls' and women's apostolic groups which it is becoming increasingly necessary to develop; in particular their work is needed in countries where, for various reasons, priests cannot effectively assume their roles as chaplain, educator, animator, and collaborator with lay apostles. Brothers can play a role similar to that of the nuns.

In collaborating with laypeople with a view to their apostolic contribution to temporal problems, in establishing contacts with men's, women's, or mixed groups, brothers and nuns will themselves complement their own formation, at the same time helping to make the whole apostolate of the Church more effective. In teaching institutions on every level, the teachers, whether religious or laypeople, must increasingly prepare their pupils for an apostolic conception of their whole life and for an authentic apostolic commitment, especially when they have finished school.

Nuns and brothers, however, must never replace the chaplain in his role as advisor or assistant in the lay apostolate. They must help him and collaborate with him. A fortiori they must be on their guard against replacing leaders and militants in the role which belongs to them. They must help the members of the movements in question to discover their apostolic mission, as much in ordinary life as in the movement itself.

May the Holy Spirit bless and enlighten the collaboration of the priesthood and the laity and, in increasing the dynamism of the Church, multiply both the number of priestly and religious vocations and the number of truly apostolic laypeople and families!

Part Four
Laypeople into Action

11
The World of the Future According
to God's Will

The problem of the lay apostolate is constantly growing greater and more urgent, as I discussed at length in Chapter Four. The whole future of the world, even the future of humanity, is at stake.

In actual fact this future is in the hands of all men, especially those who make up the masses and who are dedicated, through their daily life, to the solution of the world's problems. These are the laypeople. They must build the world in its many aspects:

Physical: by reducing material obstacles: distance, ignorance, hunger, illness, discomfort, insanitary housing; and developing its whole wealth of potential through exploration and space discoveries, scientific experiments, attempts to prolong life, etc.;

Economic and social: by working for the just and general sharing among all peoples of material goods, their production, distribution and utilisation; and in resolving the problems of big cities;

Cultural: by promoting and spreading the progress of culture through teaching, technology, art and the diffusion of ideas, and by making it more and more accessible to all people without distinction through the healthy use of leisure time;

Civic and political: by encouraging positive collaboration for the common good between peoples—and 161 furthermore, between parties and classes within a single nation—and by working in a concrete way for peace understanding, and free co-operation between those in authority and those who choose them;

Moral: by educating the different communities, families and individuals into an attitude of respect for man, for his integrity, dignity and destiny;

Religious: in ceaselessly placing all human actions and institutions at the service of God, the Creator and Redeemer, as much by the development of personal religion as by public worship.

All laypeople who are members of the Church have an apostolic mission in their lives and in the world.

The efforts that have been made during the last half century to awaken laypeople to a sense of their mission in the world have not been in vain. We must acknowledge that a great number of those who have been reached have responded enthusiastically to the discovery they have made, and we must give thanks to God for having raised up this active minority of laypeople, profoundly conscious of its responsibilities, both in the Church and in the world. But such laypeople are still too few, insufficiently enlightened, formed, courageous or committed with regard to the problems that must be tackled and the issues that are at stake.

I do not simply mean laypeople who are acting individually, step by step transforming a world which is becoming daily more paganised; I also marvel at the flowering of groups, movements, organisations and apostolic communities which are composed of and directed by laypeople who are engaged, body and soul, in the battle for the Kingdom of God. Today there are movements and organisations which cover nearly every aspect of life and action and which are eager to help their members to bear full Christian-witness. However, these are still only very humble beginnings.

In 1958 I travelled round a traditionally Catholic European country, lecturing to seminarians and priests in the various dioceses. I thought a great deal about the questions and reactions I heard from day to day and came to the conclusion that the clergy, as a whole, in spite of the repeated insistence of the Popes, has not yet understood the real content and decisive importance of the lay apostolate, or the indispensable formation it must be given, the specific methods that must be adopted and the organisation that must be promoted. Even when a large number has grasped this intellectually, many have not dared or no longer dare to commit themselves in a spirit of optimism, and many have given up their efforts after a short trial.

When I think about other trips I have made to different places in the world, or re-read the reports and the hurried notes I take down, I always arrive at this same conclusion. And it is a conclusion that any priest will reach who constantly reflects on the facts and is attentive to the echoes of this convulsed, disrupted world.

We cannot put the blame on any one person for this state of affairs. It is a responsibility which we must all shoulder together, because together we make up the Church. Thus there is all the more reason why we should judge our deficiencies and failings honestly, in the light of the tremendous possibilities that are offered us. Sincerity on this point must impel us to action, which will be the best antidote to the head-in-the-sand politics of panic and despair.

If we grasp the new dimensions which I have stressed incessantly in the course of this book the problem may seem singularly complex and oppressive; but on the other hand, the endeavour to solve it could stimulate a thrilling, unhoped for impetus.

We must admit that our timidity in developing the lay apostolate involves regrettable consequences. *The Church* loses the benefit of an inexhaustible fund of vital forces which only needs to be used and would multiply through its very use. *Laypeople* become disheartened at so often being abandoned to ignorance and impotence and as a result are in a state of mediocrity which they had not always deliberately desired. *The clergy* deprive their own apostolate of an extraordinary power of incarnation, and all too often become swamped by work which prevents them from carrying out their own tasks in the liturgy, pastoral care, Christian education, etc.

International Action suffers from an insufficient number of capable, militant Christians in new countries to collaborate with the great world-wide institutions and non-governmental organisations, and in the field of research into intelligent methods of contact with non-Christians.

It certainly happens that in their various dioceses the bishops, taken individually, each one preoccupied with the problems of the community of which he has charge, can be overwhelmed by the rapid and radical transformation of our modern world. This difficulty is shared by many of the superiors of religious orders of both men and women.

In addition to this, confusion and disorder prevail in both the concept and the organisation of apostolic work among the laity. However, if we lost heart we would in our grave responsibility. For, to give the other side of the picture, we have reached a time when there is need for research which is more and more adventurous, more searching, stubbornly tenacious and enthusiastic.

For a study of this kind more efforts must be made, both intellectually and by way of practical action. And because we are still only at the beginning, many lines of thought must be pursued, many experiments must be made, and a thousand questions must be asked.

I would need another book to develop them all, but I must content myself with a rapid enumeration of some questions that seem to me essential, in the hope that others will take up certain of my queries and give new answers to them.

The first question that must be considered is the nature of the apostolate belonging to laypeople by virtue of their lay state. Do laypeople have their own apostolate in the Church? Is this apostolate fulfilled essentially and primarily in secular life with a view to the consecration of the world? Is this 'specifically lay apostolate of the laity' dependent on the hierarchy, and if so, in what way?

If the words of Genesis, addressed to the first man and woman, are meant for all humanity, then it follows that all men must so order the world that it proclaims God's glory. Hence can it be said that all people are called to the apostolate, and since non-Christians are, in part, in possession of religious truth, have they also a share in the apostolate? Is it not an essential part of the missionary task of the Church to help them to discover and realise their own mission and to collaborate with them.

Once we start to investigate these questions, which have hitherto hardly been touched on, we quickly become aware of the great task awaiting theologians, who must work in fruitful collaboration with those who have concrete experience of apostolic life. This teamwork, in assembling and deepening the studies which have been undertaken by research workers in various countries during the last few years, should result in a real theology of temporal values and of the lay apostolate. I am certain that research into these particular questions would throw fresh and beneficial light on the theology of the Church herself.

We know that baptism and confirmation confer on the believer an explicit mission relating to the Kingdom of God. How then does it come about that there are still so few who are really committed to their own place in the providential plan? Is this call sufficiently put before them—as much, for instance, as they are invited to the state of grace or reminded of their Easter obligations?

If all laypeople were constantly alerted, encouraged and given concrete assistance in the realisation of their apostolic role, the Church would more rapidly take on a truly missionary character. Indeed we would rediscover the outlook of the early Christian Church, which was the basic inspiration behind the launching of Catholic Action: contact with people outside the Church, in order to bring them the message and person of Christ, their only true end and salvation.

The time has come to revise the fundamental concept of present-day apostolic contact. What I mean is this: is not, in principle and in fact, our apostolic action enclosed within the confines of organisations and parishes, or are we aiming beyond, to the very centre of the masses which do not belong to the Church, to the very centre of the most exposed sectors, such as the circles of the intellectuals and of those trained in new techniques and the proletarian levels of heavy industry? In short, are we concerned with educative preservation', or are we ceaselessly preparing or revising the planned projection of the Gospel into the whole of life, amongst paganised people?

Following the same train of thought, we must one day have the courage to go thoroughly into the question of the layperson's role in regard to all those who belong to other religions, Christian or non-Christian. Laypeople in temporal life are in the front lines of action: they are confronted with the most widely differing ideologies, both religious and materialistic. Whatever their particular sphere may be their secular activities place them there in the most natural way. Are their everyday contacts transformed into apostolic contacts? Is this a real collaboration with the work of God, keeping pace with the questioners who are always at their side? Are laypeople conscious and prepared?

Thus, the apostolate of the laity, seen in all its dynamic dimensions, puts the whole missionary action of the Church in a new light: we can no longer be content to send priests and nuns into so-called mission fields'. Every Christian must be given the responsibility in his own environment of planting the Church wherever she does not exist. If all people truly lived this mission, what marvellous reserves of apostolic energy would be unleashed; what a dazzling spiritual rebirth would come about in Christian communities wholeheartedly responding to the total dimensions of the Church's mission.

Today people are making a multitude of distinctions between action and apostolate; the apostolate of Catholics and Catholic

Action; the direct and the indirect apostolate; between the apostolate in the strict sense and in a more general sense; and many others as well. Such distinctions need to be made, and progressively more light must be thrown on this part of the Church's life which can still be said to be on very uncertain ground. This is quite normal, because the uncertain ground is life itself. But still, I believe that this is not enough.

Christians will never transform their ordinary lives into an apostolate, their apostolic action will never attain the desired-for influence and results, unless they are helped by a form of organisation which is on one hand a powerful impulse to the apostolate, and on the other, co-ordinates its many efforts while keeping to a vision of the whole.

Important research should be undertaken concerning the value of apostolic organisations. Which among them realise an authentic apostolate? Which are primary, essential? And within the organisations themselves, which of their aspects, methods and activities gives them their genuinely apostolic character? Consequently, which are the secondary organisations, or those which will have to change?

We must go even further than this. Confronted with the mass of human problems which must be faced and coped with in future, confronted with the vast apostolic task which continually exceeds the established limits and has repercussions on an increasingly larger scale— national, continental, world wide—the Church must consider the problem of the lay apostolate in its entirety in order to develop this apostolate more efficiently. Today, in all kinds of circles, people are discussing the eventual creation of a new Roman dicastery, a secretariat, a pontifical commission or similar institution which will consider all the problems relative to study, organisation and formation in the field of the lay apostolate. Will these wishes and hopes materialise?

While such an institution must be created, it is absolutely essential that its conception and function should be studied with the greatest care, so that, in the field of action as in the field of formation, the primary aim of the lay apostolate is safeguarded: an apostolate which is achieved fundamentally in and through human beings, in the very heart of the life of the world. We must always be conscious of that dynamic power, a power which must be developed, which starts with the humblest at the very base of the Church and rises to its heights through the inspiration of the Holy Spirit. I thank thee, Father, said

Christ when his disciples came back from their first mission, 'that thou hast hidden these tidings from the wise and understanding and revealed them to babes . . .' (Luke 10:21).

Yes, we need a central institution, but one which animates, encourages, breathes life, stifles nothing and kills nothing. Variety, and, to a certain extent, liberty in the organisation of the apostolate will always be a source and sign of spiritual riches in the Church which correspond to the riches of life itself.

Finally, to come back to the question which I believe to be essential: have we decided to form laypeople, all laypeople, with a view to their apostolate? Or, perhaps we should first ask: do we believe that all laypeople need formation, that they are fully qualified to receive it, and that everything possible should be done to give it to them?

To carry out this eminently evangelical and educative work, we must use all the people and institutions, all the time and the methods that we need. Everyone in the Church must be ready to make the maximum effort to assume this joint task: parents, schools, clergy, parish communities, organisations, the press, audiovisual techniques. All this is on the secular level, just as the Church is in charge of priestly vocations, seminaries, the extension of missionary activities.

We must realise that, at present we are sadly wide of the mark. More specifically, we must consider what part the priest will play in the future in apostolic formation, and how much of his daily time he can give to help those who are involved. Before such considerations, however, the respective roles of priest and layperson must be more clearly defined. Priests must be more ready to accord laypeople their total responsibility as Christian adults in their own domain, while becoming themselves more fully dedicated to their priestly mission as the animators and educators of the lay apostolate. This must come about through intimate supernatural collaboration which is based on complete reciprocal trust.

This is an unheard of opportunity for the clergy to spread the radiance of the Christian mission in the world of today. Whether or not it will be seized as a special grace providentially offered to the Church in these difficult times will depend to a very large extent on the response of the priesthood.

Above all else, laypeople, after the apostolic experience of the last twenty-five years, are buoyed with the highest hope. They expect something of the Church and, more particularly and immediately, of the Council. They desire the Church, through her most responsible authorities, to confirm them solemnly in their mission, proclaiming the value the Church attaches to their own apostolate in temporal life and institutions, and her desire to see them become more fully and deeply committed to it.

Now more than ever—thanks to the unification of the world through scientific and technical progress, as well as to the dangers which stimulated this progress—the world is waiting for the Church, for the realisation of her mission through the grace of Christ. This world must be consecrated by laypeople.

The Church is waiting for laypeople, but what does she expect of them?

This is the question that obsesses me when I meditate on that sentence of Pius XII, which is like a watchword given to the young workers of the YCW and through them to the laypeople of the whole world: 'Build a world according to Gods will!'[33]

An immense, a superhuman task lies before us. It makes its own' demands. A battle is not won without the infantry; great modern structures are not built without bulldozers. We must all have the courage to undertake this work, to whatever level of society we belong, wherever we are placed on the surface of the globe. We must forge ahead with an exploring, pioneering spirit, not afraid of groping in the dark, of running risks, of retreating in order to advance, not afraid to stop and think, to listen to what life and experience teaches us. We must have a fearless spirit, because the Church has all the graces promised by her divine Founder to spread her messianic message throughout the world, a message truer and more powerful than all the ideologies c present, past or future. 'The spirit breathes where h will . . .'

May we too make our own, in spirit and in truth, thos stanzas of the Prophet, so full of hope:

> 'Fear not, for I am with you; . . .
> Everyone who is called by my name,
> Whom I created for my glory,
> Whom I formed and made.'
> (Isaiah 43:5–7)

---

33. . Speech on 25 August 1957.

'Lift up your eyes round about and see;
They all gather together, they come to you;
Your sons shall come from far,
And your daughters shall be carried in the arms.
Then you shall see and be radiant, Your heart shall thrill and rejoice;
Because the abundance of the sea shall be turned to you,
The wealth of the nations shall come to you.'
(Isaiah 60:4–5)

'The people whom I formed for myself: shall show forth my praise!'
(Isaiah 43:21)

'And from them I will send survivors to the nations . . .
And they shall declare my glory among the nations.'

And they shall bring all your brethren from all the nations
As an offering to the Lord, . . .
And some of them also
I will take for priests and for Levites, says the Lord.'
(Isaiah 66:19–21)

Epilogue

I have tried in this book to outline the essential points in the development of my thought and research on what I consider to be one of the greatest and most crucial issues of the Church in our time: to set her potential of living forces into action through the development of the lay apostolate.

There are many gaps, many repetitions to be found in these pages. People will say too that I have not revealed anything new, or else that my subject has been better expressed by others. All this will be true. And it is quite true too that I have been saying the same thing all though my life I What is more, I'm not sorry. It is not the launching of new ideas that counts, but the search for the Kingdom of God. And this, with the means given me, is simply what I have tried to do in my priestly ministry among laypeople.

But today I must stress again, with the utmost force, what my conscience considers to be the will of God: *the world needs lay apostles and the Church must form them!*

People have been wondering whether or not to talk about a failure of Catholic Action. My reply to this is that the emphasis of the question is wrongly placed. My whole experience has shown me that we should rather be asking ourselves: 'Have we wanted and prepared, in every possible way, an authentic lay apostolate?'

There is neither a sense of failure nor a sense of victory, but a very great hope in the hearts of all Christians, and in the heart of their Mother, the Church. For Christ has already overcome the world.

For myself, I am resolutely optimistic about the future.

Our fundamental goal is a lay apostolate, with all its deepest needs and demands. To those who hesitate, who are afraid of laypeople—mature laypeople—I say: 'You must believe in them, and believe in them loyally.' Faith is the first and essential condition of the awakening of laypeople. Faith which puts its trust in the grace of the Holy Spirit and the charity it diffuses in every human heart.

We are only now taking the first faltering steps in our effort to promote the lay apostolate in the Church. Everything I have said in this book is the secret' of my priestly life: a secret that I have constantly repeated— that I have shouted—from every public place.

This is nothing other than the secret of the Church, who calls all her sons, in the name of Christ, to accomplish her unique mission.

It is also the secret of the commitment of thousands and thousands of laypeople, who, hearing this call and discovering its sublime grandeur, have unhesitatingly committed their whole lives to the service of Christ and their brothers in the apostolic adventure.

And through the interplay of a divine, irreversible solidarity between priest and laity, it was often the vision of their commitment which stimulated, sustained, nourished and inspired my incessant research.

Glory be to the Father, and to the Son and to the Holy Ghost.

Brussels, September, 1962.

CPSIA information can be obtained
at www.ICGtesting.com
Printed in the USA
BVHW090105100222
628352BV00008B/203